William Cunningham Glen

The Elementary Education Act, 1870

With introduction, notes, and index, and appendix containing the inforporrated statutes

William Cunningham Glen

The Elementary Education Act, 1870
With introduction, notes, and index, and appendix containing the inforporrated statutes

ISBN/EAN: 9783337218768

Printed in Europe, USA, Canada, Australia, Japan

Cover: Foto ©Suzi / pixelio.de

THE

ELEMENTARY EDUCATION ACT, 1870,

WITH

INTRODUCTION, NOTES, AND INDEX,

AND

APPENDIX CONTAINING THE INCORPORATED STATUTES.

BY

W. CUNNINGHAM GLEN,

BARRISTER-AT-LAW.

LONDON:
SHAW AND SONS, FETTER LANE,
Law Printers and Publishers.

1870.

LONDON: PRINTED BY SHAW AND SONS, FETTER LANE.

PREFACE.

The Elementary Education Act, 1870, is a statute which is calculated, more than any other of recent times to elevate the masses of the people; and is the result of many years agitation by the various religious denominations and political parties in the State. The object which it will accomplish may be stated in a very few words. It will place an elementary school wherever there is a child to be taught, whether of rich or poor parents: and it will compel every parent and guardian of a child to have it taught, at least, the rudiments of education, and that without reference to any religious creed or persuasion.

The Editor, at the request of the Publishers, has prepared the present work, and trusts that it will be found to be a useful and practical guide to all those who may be called upon officially or otherwise to bring the Act into operation. In the Appendix will be found all the Incorporated Acts, besides other useful information.

The work is prefaced by an Introduction, containing a general *resumé* of the provisions of the Act; and the importance of a voluminous Index has not been overlooked.

5, Elm Court, Temple,
1st September, 1870.

CONTENTS.

THE ELEMENTARY EDUCATION ACT, 1870.

FIRST SCHEDULE.

SECOND SCHEDULE.

First Part.

Second Part.

Third Part.

THIRD SCHEDULE.

FOURTH SCHEDULE.

FIFTH SCHEDULE.

APPENDIX.

I. SCHOOL SITES ACTS.

II. Charitable Trusts Acts.

INTRODUCTION.

The districts in which elementary schools (that is, schools at which the children attend from the homes of their parents, and charge is taken of them during the school hours only) are to be established are,—the Metropolis within the jurisdiction of the Metropolitan Board of Works; municipal boroughs; the district of the Oxford Local Board of Health; and elsewhere, in all parishes in England and Wales. For each district a school board is to be established, and the expenses of the board in excess of the school fees are to be paid out of local rates.

There shall be provided for every school district a sufficient amount of accommodation in public elementary schools, available for all children resident in the district for whose elementary education efficient and suitable provision is not otherwise made.

Where the education department are satisfied, and have given public notice that there is an insufficient amount of public school accommodation for any school district, and the deficiency is not supplied, a school board shall be formed for the district, and shall supply the deficiency, and in case of default the education department shall cause it to be done.

Every public elementary school shall be conducted in accordance with the following regulations:—(1.) It shall not be required, as a condition of any child being admitted into or continuing in the school, that he shall attend or abstain from attending any Sunday school, or any place of religious worship, or that he shall attend any religious observance or any instruction in religious subjects in the school or elsewhere, from which observance or instruction he may be withdrawn by his parent, or that he shall, if withdrawn by his parent, attend the school on any day exclusively set apart for religious observance by the religious body to which his parent belongs:—(2.) The time or times during which any religious observance is practised or instruction in religious subjects is given at any meeting of the school shall be either at the beginning or at the end, or at the beginning and the end of such meeting, and shall be inserted in a time table to be approved by the education department, and kept permanently and conspicuously affixed in every school room; and any scholar may be withdrawn by his parent from such observance or instruction without forfeiting any of the other benefits of the school:—(3.) the school shall be open at all times to the inspection of any of Her Majesty's inspectors, so, however, that it shall be no part of the duties of such inspector to inquire into any instruction in religious subjects given at such school, or to examine any scholar therein in religious knowlege or in any religious subject or book:—(4.) the school shall be conducted in accordance with the conditions required to be fulfilled by an elementary school in order to obtain an annual parliamentary grant.

For the purpose of determining the amount of public school accommodation, required for the district, the education department shall, immediately after the passing of the Act, cause returns to be made to them, and on receiving them, and after such inquiry as they think necessary, shall consider whether any and what public school accommodation is required for the district, and in so doing they shall take into consideration every school, whether actually situated in the school district or not, which in their opinion will be suitable for the children of the district.

When the department have done so, they shall publish a notice of their decision, setting forth with respect to the district the description, number, size, and description of the schools available for the district which they have taken into consideration, and the amount and description of the accommodation, which appears to them to be required, and any other particulars which they think expedient.

If any persons being either ratepayers of the district, not less than ten, or, if less than ten, being rated to the poor rate upon a rateable value of not less than one-third of the whole rateable value of the district, or the managers of any elementary school in the district, feel aggrieved by the decision of the department, they may, within one month after the publication of the notice, apply for a public inquiry to take place.

At any time after the expiration of the month, if no public inquiry is directed, or after the receipt of the report made after the inquiry, the department may, if they think that the amount of public school accommodation for the district is insufficient, publish a final notice, directing that the accommodation mentioned in it as required be supplied.

If after the expiration of a limited time, not exceeding six months, the department are satisfied that all the accommodation required by the final notice has not been so supplied, nor is in course of being supplied with due despatch, they shall cause a school board to be formed for the district, and shall send a requisition to the board requiring them to take proceedings forthwith for supplying the school accommodation mentioned in the requisition.

If the school board fail to comply with the requisition within twelve months, they shall be deemed to be in default, and the department may then proceed as in the case of a school board in default.

Where application is made to the department with respect to any school district by the persons who, if there were a school board in the district, would elect the board, or with respect to any borough, by the council; or where the department are satisfied that the managers of any elementary school in any district are unable or unwilling any longer to maintain such school, and that if the school is discontinued the amount of public school accommodation for the district will be insufficient, the department may, after inquiry, cause a school board to be formed for the district, and send a requisition to the board in the same manner in all respects as if they had published a final notice. An application for these purposes may be made by a resolution passed by the electing body after notice published at least a week previously, or by the council.

After the receipt of any returns subsequently to the first with respect to any district, and after inquiry, the department shall consider whether any and what school accommodation is required in the district, in the same manner as in the case of the first returns; and where in the district there is no school board they may issue notices and take proceedings in the same manner as they may after the receipt of the first returns; and where there is a school board they shall proceed in manner which the Act directs.

Every school provided by a school board shall be conducted under the control and management of the board in accordance with the following regulations:—(1.) The school shall be a public elementary school:—(2.) No religious catechism or religious formulary which is distinctive of any particular denomination shall be taught in the school.

The board may from time to time delegate any of their powers, except the power of raising money, and in particular may delegate the control and management of any school, with or without any conditions or restrictions, to a body of managers appointed by them, consisting of not less than three persons. They may from time to time remove all or any of the managers, and, within the above limit, add to or diminish the number of or otherwise alter the constitution or powers of the body of managers. Any manager may resign on giving written notice to the board; and the schedule to the Act contains rules respecting the proceedings of bodies of managers so appointed.

If the school board do or permit any act in contravention of or fail to comply with the regulations according to which a school provided by them is required to be conducted, the education department may declare the board to be a board in default, and may proceed accordingly; and every act or omission of any member of the board, or manager, or any person under the control of the board, shall be deemed to be permitted by the board, unless the contrary be proved. If any dispute arises as to whether the board have done or permitted any act in contravention of or have failed to comply with the regulations, the matter shall be referred to the department, whose decision shall be final.

Every child attending a school provided by any school board shall pay such weekly fee as may be prescribed by the board, with the consent of the department; but the board may from time to time, for a renewable period not exceeding six months, remit the whole or any part of the school fee in the case of any child when they are of opinion that the parent of such child is unable from poverty to pay the same, but such remission shall not be deemed to be parochial relief given to the parent.

The board shall maintain and keep efficient every school provided by them, and shall from time to time provide such additional school accommodation as is, in their opinion, necessary in order to supply a sufficient amount of public school accommodation for their district, and the board may discontinue any school, or change the site of any school, if they satisfy the department that the school to be discontinued is unnecessary, or that the change of site is expedient. If at any time the department are satisfied that a school board have failed to perform their duty, either by not maintaining or keeping efficient every school provided by them, or by not providing such additional school accommodation as is necessary in order to supply a sufficient amount of public school accommodation in their district, the department may send them a requisition requiring them to fulfil the duty which they have failed to perform; and if the board fail within the time limited, not being less than three months, to comply therewith to the satisfaction of the department, the board shall be deemed to be a school board in default, and the education department may proceed accordingly.

Every school board for the purpose of providing sufficient public school accommodation for their district, whether in obedience to any requisition or not, may provide, by building or otherwise, schoolhouses properly fitted up, and improve, enlarge, and fit up any schoolhouse provided by them, and supply school apparatus and everything necessary for the efficiency of the schools, and purchase and take on lease any land, and any right over land. With respect to the purchase of land by school boards the Lands Clauses Consolidation Act, 1845, and the Acts amending the same are incorporated. The school board, however, before putting in force any of the powers of those Acts with respect to the purchase and taking of land otherwise than by agreement, shall conform to the regulations of the Act in that respect, and may afterwards present a petition under their seal to the education department, for an order to put in force the powers of the Acts with respect to the purchase and taking of land otherwise than by agreement. If, on consideration of the petition and proof of the publication and service of the proper notices, the department think fit to proceed with the case, they may appoint some person to inquire in the district in which the land is situate respecting the propriety of the proposed order, and also direct such person to hold a public inquiry: after such consideration and proof, and after receiving a report made upon the inquiry, the department may make the order prayed for, either absolutely or with such conditions and modifications as they may think fit; and it shall be the duty of the school board to serve a copy of the order upon the persons affected by it; but no such order shall be of any validity unless it has been confirmed by Act of parliament.

The School Sites Acts shall apply in the same manner as if the school board were trustees or managers of a school board; and land may be acquired under any of these Acts, or partly under one and partly under another Act.

For the purpose of the purchase by the managers of any public elementary school of a schoolhouse, or a site for one, "The Lands Clauses Consolidation Act, 1845," and the Acts amending the same, (except so much as relates to the purchase of land otherwise than by agreement,) are also incorporated with the Act, and land may be acquired under the Incorporated Acts, or under the School Sites Acts, or any of them, or partly under one and partly under another Act. Any persons desirous of establishing a public elementary school shall be deemed to be managers, if they obtain the approval of the education department to the establishment of the school.

The provisions of the Charitable Trusts Acts, 1853 to 1869, which relate to the sale, leasing, and exchange of lands belonging to any charity, are made to extend to the sale, leasing, and exchange of the whole or any part of any land or schoolhouse belonging to a school board which may not be required by the board.

The managers of any elementary school in the district of a school board may arrange for transferring their school to the school board with the consent of the education department; and, if there are annual subscribers to the school, with the consent of a majority, not being less than two-thirds in number of those present at a meeting duly summoned for the purpose, and who vote on the question.

After the expiration of six months from the date of the transfer the consent of the education department shall be conclusive evidence that the arrangement has been made in conformity with the Act, and the arrangement may provide for the future interest the board shall have in the school.

When an arrangement is made the managers may, whether the legal interest in the schoolhouse or endowment is vested in them or in some person as trustee for them or the school, convey to the board all such interest in the schoolhouse and endowment as is vested in them or in such trustee, or such smaller interest as may be required under the arrangement.

Where any school or any interest therein has been transferred by the managers to the school board of any district the board may, by a resolution and with the consent of the education department, re-transfer such school or such interest therein to a body of managers, and upon such re-transfer may convey all the interest in the school-house and in any endowment belonging to the school vested in the board.

The school board may, from time to time, for a renewable period not exceeding six months, pay the whole or any part of the school fees payable at any public elementary school by any child resident in their district whose parent is in their opinion unable from poverty to pay such fees; but no such payment shall be made or refused on condition of the child attending any public elementary school other than such as may be selected by the parent; and the payment shall not be deemed to be parochial relief.

If a school board satisfy the education department that, on the ground of the poverty of the inhabitants of any place in their district, it is expedient for the interests of education to provide a school at which no fees shall be required from the scholars, the board may, subject to such rules and conditions as the department may prescribe, provide such school, and may admit scholars to it without requiring any fee.

A school board shall have the same powers of contributing money in the case of an industrial school as is given to a prison authority by "The Industrial Schools Act, 1866;" and upon the election of a school board in a borough the council of that borough shall cease to have power to contribute to an industrial school, and a school board may establish a certified industrial school, and shall for that purpose have the same powers as they have for the purpose of providing sufficient school accommodation for their district; but the board shall be subject to the jurisdiction of one of Her Majsty's principal secretaries of state in the same manner as the managers of any other industrial school are subject, and the school shall be subject to the provisions of that Act, and not of the Elementary Education Act.

The school board shall be elected, in a borough, by the persons whose names are on the burgess roll of such borough; and in a parish not situate in the metropolis by the ratepayers.

At every election every voter shall be entitled to a number of votes equal to the number of the members of the board to be elected, and may give all such votes to one candidate, or may distribute them among the candidates, as he thinks fit.

The school board shall be a body corporate, and no act or proceeding of the board shall be questioned on account of any vacancy or vacancies in their body, and no disqualification of or defect in the election of any persons or person acting as members or member of the board shall be deemed to vitiate any proceedings of the board in which they or he have taken part, in cases where the majority of members parties to such proceedings were duly entitled to act.

The members of a school board may apply any money in their hands for the purpose of indemnifying themselves against any law costs or damages which they may incur in or in consequence of the execution of the powers granted to them.

Further rules are contained in the Act with respect to the proceedings of school boards, except in the metropolis. The number of members of a school board shall be such number, not less than five nor more than fifteen, as may be determined by the education department, and afterwards from time to time by a resolution of the board approved by the department.

The department may, at any time after the date at which they are authorized to cause a school board to be formed, send a requisition to the mayor requiring him to take such proceedings; and in case of default some person appointed by the department may take such proceedings, and shall have for that purpose the same powers as the person in default.

If from any cause in any school district the school board either are not elected at the time fixed for the first election, or at any time cease to be in existence, or to be of sufficient number to form a quorum, or neglect or refuse to act, the department may proceed in the same manner as if the board were in default.

In case any question arises as to the right of any person to act as a member of a school board, the education department may, if they think fit, inquire into the circumstances of the case, and make order thereon.

No member of a board, and no manager, shall hold or accept any place of profit the appointment to which is vested in the board or in any managers, nor shall in any way share or be concerned in the profits of any bargain or contract with the board or managers; except as to any sale of land or loan of money to a school board, any bargain or contract made with or work done by a company in which such member holds shares, or the insertion of any advertisement relating to the affairs of the board in any newspaper in which such member has a share or interest, provided he do not vote with respect to such sale, loan, bargain, contract, work, or insertion, under a penalty not exceeding fifty pounds.

A school board may appoint a clerk and a treasurer and other necessary officers, including teachers, to hold office during the pleasure of the board, and may assign them salaries or other remuneration, and may from time to time remove any of such officers. Two or more boards may arrange for the appointment of the same person to be an officer to both or all.

Every school board may appoint an officer to enforce any byelaws under the Act with reference to the attendance of children at school, and to bring children who are liable under the Industrial Schools Act, 1866, to be sent to a certified industrial school before two justices in order to their being so sent.

The provisions of the Act with respect to the formation and the election of school boards in boroughs and parishes shall not extend to the metropolis. A school board in the metropolis shall consist of such number of members elected by the ten parliamentary divisions into which it is divided, as the education department may by order fix, and the department, as soon as may be, shall by order determine the boundaries of such divisions for the purposes of the Act, and the number of members to be elected by each: the provisions already mentioned with respect to the constitution of the school board shall extend to the constitution of the school board in the metropolis, and the name of the school board shall be the School Board for London: elections shall take place in the month of November every third year on the day from time to time appointed by the school board: at every election, every voter shall be entitled to a number of votes equal to the number of the members of the board to be elected for the division, and may give all such votes to one candidate, or may distribute them among the candidates, as he thinks fit: the members of the board shall, in the city of London, be elected by the same persons and in like manner as common councilmen are elected, and in the other divisions by the same persons and in the same manner as vestrymen under The Metropolis Management Act, 1855. The school board shall proceed at once to supply their district with sufficient public school accommodation, and any requisition sent by the education department to such board may relate to any of the divisions in like manner as if it were a school district. A chairman of the school board shall be elected either from the members of the board or not, and any chairman who is not an elected member of the board shall, by virtue of his office, be a member of the board as if he had been so elected. The school board shall apportion the amount required to be raised to meet the deficiency in the school fund among the different parts of the metropolis in proportion to their rateable value. For obtaining payment of the amount, the board have the like powers as the Metropolitan Board of Works have for obtaining payment of any sum assessed by them on the same part of the metropolis.

The school board for London may pay to their chairman such salary as they may from time to time, with the sanction of the education department, fix.

If at any time application is made to the education department by the school board for London, or by any six members, and it is shown to the satisfaction of the department that the population of any of the divisions mentioned, as shown by any census taken under the authority of Parliament, has varied materially from that shown by the previous census, or that the rateable value of any of the divisions has materially varied from the rateable value of the same division ten years previously, the department, after inquiry may make an order altering, by way of increase or decrease, the number of members of that and any other division.

Where the education department are of opinion that it would be expedient to form a school district larger than a borough or a parish, they may, except in the metropolis, by order made after such inquiry and notice, form a united school district by uniting any two or more adjoining school districts, and upon such union cause a school board to be formed for the united district.

The department may cause inquiry to be made into the expediency of uniting any two or more districts, and if after inquiry they are of opinion that it would be expedient to unite any such districts, they shall in the notice of their decision as to the public school accommodation, state that they propose to unite such district. The order for the union may be made at the time when the department are first authorised to cause a school board to be formed or subsequently.

The education department may, by order made after inquiry and notice dissolve a united school district, and may deal with the constituent district thereof, in the same manner as if they had never been united, and may cause school boards to be elected therein.

The school board for a limited district shall be such number of members elected by the electors of the district as may be specified in the order forming the district, subject to alteration in the same manner as in the case of any other school board; and every person who in any of the districts would be entitled if the district were not united to vote at the election of members of a school board for such constituent district shall be an elector, and the provisions of the Act respecting the election of a board in a district shall extend to the election of such members.

If the department are of opinion that any parish in a united district has too few ratepayers to be entitled to act as a separate parish for the purposes of the Act, they may by order direct that it shall for the purpose of voting for a member or members of the school board, and for all or any of the purposes of the Act, be added to another parish.

The education department may direct that one school district shall contribute towards the provision or maintenance of public elementary schools in another district or districts, and in such case the district shall pay to the school owning district or districts, a proportion of the expenses of such provision or maintenance. Where one district contributes to the provision or maintenance of any school in another district, such number of persons as the department direct shall be elected in the contributing district, and shall be members of the board of the school owning district, but that district shall, except, so far as regards the raising of money and the attendance of children at school, be deemed alone to be the district of such school board.

The school boards of any two or more school districts with the sanction of the education department, may combine together for any purpose relating to elementary schools, and in particular may combine for the purpose of providing, maintaining, and keeping efficient schools common to such districts.

The expenses of the school board shall be paid out of a fund called the school fund. There shall be carried to the school fund all moneys received as fees from scholars, or out of moneys provided by parliament, or raised by way of loan, or in any manner whatever received by the school board. Any sum required to meet any deficiency in the school fund, whether for satisfying past or future liabilities, shall be paid by the rating authority out of the local rate.

In a united district the school board shall apportion the amount required to meet the deficiency in the school and among the districts constituting such united district in proportion to the rateable value of each such constituent district, and may raise the same by a precept sent to the rating authority of each constituent district. Where one school district contributes to the expenses of the schools in another school district, the authority of the school owning district may send their precept either to the school board, if any, or to the rating authority of the contributing district, requiring them to pay to their treasurer the amount therein specified.

If the rating authority of any place make default in paying the amount specified in any precept of the school board; or where a school board require to raise a sum from any place which is part of a parish, then without prejudice to any other remedy, the school board may appoint an officer or officers to act within such place, and to make and levy rates to satisfy their precepts.

Where a school board incur any expense in providing or enlarging a schoolhouse, they may, with the consent of the education department, spread the payment over several years, not exceeding fifty, and may for that purpose borrow money on the security of the school fund and local rate. They may, if they so agree with the mortgagee, pay the amount borrowed, with the interest, by equal annual instalments, not exceeding fifty, and if they do not so agree, they shall annually set aside one-fiftieth of the sum borrowed as a sinking fund. For the purpose of such borrowing the clauses of "The Commissioners Clauses Act, 1847," with respect to the mortgages to be executed by the commissioners are incorporated with the Act.

The Public Works Loan Commissioners are empowered to lend any money required on the security of the school fund and local rate, and the loan shall be repaid within a period not exceeding fifty years, at 3½ per cent. interest; but any sum borrowed by the school board for London, may be borrowed from and may be lent by the Metropolitan Board of Works.

The accounts of the school board shall be made up and

balanced to the 25th March and 29th September in every year.

The accounts are to be audited by the auditor of accounts relating to the relief of the poor for the audit district in which the school district is situate. The audit will be conducted as near as may be in like manner as a poor-law audit; and the Poor Law Board may from time to time make such regulations as may be necessary respecting the form of keeping the accounts and the audit of them.

Where the education department are, after inquiry, satisfied that a school board is in default, they may by order declare such board to be in default, and by the same or any other order appoint any persons, not less than five or more than fifteen, to be members of such school board, and may from time to time remove any member so appointed, and fill up any vacancy in the number of members, and add to or diminish the number of such members. After the date of the order of appointment the persons who were previously members of the board shall be deemed to have vacated their offices as if they were dead; but any such member may be appointed a member by the education department.

Where a school board is not elected at the time fixed for the first election, or has ceased to be in existence, the department may proceed in the same manner as if the board had been elected and were in existence.

The expenses incurred in the performance of their duties by the persons appointed by the department to be members of a school board, including such remuneration as the department may assign to them, shall, together with all expenses incurred by the board, be paid out of the school fund; and any deficiency in the school fund may be raised by the school board as provided by the Act.

Where the members of a school board have been appointed by the department, such school board shall not borrow or charge the school fund with the principal and interest of any loan exceeding such amount as the department certify to be required

Where the department are of opinion that in the case of any district the school board are in default, or are not properly performing their duties, they may by order direct that the then members of the school board shall vacate their seats, and that the vacancies shall be filled by a new election; and after the date fixed by any such order the then members shall be deemed to have vacated their seats, and a new election shall be held in the same manner, and the department shall take the same proceedings for the purpose of such election as if it were the first election; but the education department shall cause to be laid before both Houses of Parliament in every year a special report in respect of any such proceeding.

On or before the 1st January, 1871, or in the case of the metropolis before the expiration of four months from the date of the election of the chairman of the school board, every local authority, and subsequently any such local authority whenever required by the education department, but not oftener than once in every year, shall send to the department a return containing such particulars with respect to the elementary schools and children requiring elementary education in their district as the department may from time to time require. For the purpose of obtaining such returns the department shall draw up forms, and supply to the local authority such number of forms as may be required; and the managers or principal teacher of every school shall fill up the form, and return the same to the local authority within the time specified in that behalf.

The returns shall be made in the metropolis by the school board, in boroughs by the council, and in every parish not situated in a borough or the metropolis by persons appointed for the purpose, or by the overseers. Where a board is formed, the returns shall be made by such school board within their district.

If any local authority fail to make the returns, the education department may appoint any person or persons to make such returns, and the person or persons so appointed shall for that purpose have the the same powers and authorities as the local authority. And the department may appoint any persons to act as inspectors of returns, who shall proceed to inquire into the accuracy and completeness of any one or more returns, and into the efficiency and suitability of any school mentioned in any such return, or which ought to have been mentioned, and to inspect and examine the scholars in every such school, or examine the school books and registers, or make copies or extracts therefrom, such school shall not be taken into consideration among the schools giving efficient elementary education to the district.

Where a public inquiry is held the education department shall appoint some person who shall proceed to hold the inquiry, and the person so appointed shall for that purpose hold a sitting or sittings in some convenient place in the neighbourhood of the school district to which the subject of inquiry relates, and thereat shall hear, receive, and examine any evidence and information offered, and hear and inquire into any objections or representations made respecting the subject of inquiry, with power from time to time to adjourn any sitting. Notice shall be published of every such sitting (except an adjourned sitting) seven days at least before holding it.

The person appointed shall make a report in writing to the education department setting forth the result of the inquiry, and stating his opinion on the subject thereof, and his reasons for such opinion, and the objections and representations, if any, made on the inquiry, and his opinion thereon: and the department shall cause a copy of such report to be deposited with the school board (if any), or, if there is none, the town clerk of the borough, or the churchwardens or overseers of the parishes to which the inquiry relates, and may make an order directing that the costs of the proceedings and inquiry shall be paid, according as they think just, or they may before ordering the inquiry to be held, require the applicants to give security for such expenses, and in case of refusal may refuse to order the inquiry to be held.

Every school board may from time to time, with the approval of the education department, make byelaws for all or any of the following purposes: requiring the parents of children of such age, not less than five years nor more than thirteen years, as may be fixed by the byelaws to cause such children (unless there is some reasonable excuse) to attend school. Determining the time during which children are so to attend school; provided that no such byelaw shall prevent the withdrawal of any child from any religious observance or instruction in religious subjects, or shall require any child to attend school on any day exclusively set apart for religious observance by the religious body to which his parent belongs, or shall be contrary to anything contained in any Act for regulating the education of children employed in labour. Providing for the remission or payment of the whole or any part of the fees of any child where the parent satisfies the school board that he is unable from poverty to pay the same. Imposing penalties for the breach of any byelaws. Revoking or altering any byelaw previously made.

Any byelaw requiring a child between ten and thirteen years of age to attend school shall provide for the total or partial exemption of such child from the obligation to attend school if one of Her Majesty's inspectors certifies that such child has reached a standard of education specified in such byelaw. Any of the following reasons shall be a reasonable excuse for non-attendance at school: 1. That the child is under efficient instruction in some other manner: 2. That the child has been prevented from attending school by sickness or any unavoidable cause: 3. That there is no public elementary school open which the child can attend within such distance, not exceeding three miles, measured according to the nearest road from the residence of such child, as the byelaws may prescribe.

Where any school or any endowment of a school was excepted from the Endowed Schools Act, 1869, on the ground that such school was at the commencement of that Act in receipt of an annual parliamentary grant, the governing body of such school or endowment may frame and submit to the education department a scheme respecting such school or endowment, who may approve such scheme with or without any modifications as they think fit. The same powers may be exercised by means of such scheme as may be exercised by means of any scheme under the Endowed Schools Act, 1869;

and when approved by the education department, shall have effect as if it were a scheme made under that Act.

Where the managers of any public elementary school not provided by a school board desire to have their school inspected or the scholars therein examined, as well in respect of religious as of other subjects, by an inspector other than one of Her Majesty's inspectors, such managers may, after public notice, fix a day or days not exceeding two in any one year for such inspection or examination. On any such day any religious observance may be practised, and any instruction in religious subjects given at any time during the meeting of the school, but any scholar who has been withdrawn by his parent from any religious observance or instruction in religious subjects shall not be required to attend the school on any such day.

Where a parish is situated partly within and partly without a borough, the part situate outside of the borough shall be taken to be for all the purposes of the Act, a parish by itself, and the ratepayers thereof may meet in vestry in the same manner in all respects as if they were the inhabitants of a parish.

The rateable value of any parish or school district shall for the purposes of the Act be the rateable value as stated in the valuation lists, if any, and if there are none, then as stated in the rate book for the time being in force in such parish and in the parishes constituting the district; and the overseers and other persons having the custody of such valuation lists and rate book are required to produce them to the school board.

Notices and other matters required by the Act to be published shall, unless otherwise expressly provided, be published,—1. By advertisement in some one or more of the newspapers circulating in the district. 2. By causing a copy to be affixed, during not less than twelve hours in the day, on Sunday, on or near the principal doors of every church and chapel in the district, and certificates and all documents required by the Act to be served or sent may, unless otherwise expressly provided, be served and sent by post. Certificates and other documents may be served on a school board by serving the same on their clerk, or by sending the same to or delivering the same at the office of such board, and certificates and other documents may be in writing or in print, or partly in both, and if requiring authentication by a school board may be signed by their clerk.

All orders and documents of the education department, if purporting to be signed by some secretary or assistant secretary of the department, shall, until the contrary is proved, be deemed to have been so signed and to have been made by the education department, and may be proved by the production of a copy thereof purporting to have been so signed, and the Documentary Evidence Act, 1868, shall apply to the education department, and after the expiration of three months from the date of any order or requisition of the department no objection to the legality thereof shall be entertained in any legal proceeding whatever.

A school board may appear in all legal proceedings by their clerk, or by some member of the board duly authorized.

The provisions of the School Sites Acts with respect to the tenure of the office of the schoolmaster or schoolmistress, and to the recovery of possession of any premises held over by a master or mistress who has been dismissed or ceased to hold office, shall extend to the case of any school provided by a school board, and of any master or mistress of such school, in the same manner as if the school board were the trustees or managers of the school as mentioned in those Acts.

Every ratepayer in a school district may at all reasonable times, without payment, inspect and take copies of and extracts from all books and documents belonging to or under the control of the school board, and any person who hinders a ratepayer from doing so, or demands a fee for allowing him so to do, shall be liable, on summary conviction, to a penalty not exceeding five pounds for each offence.

If any returning officer, clerk, or other person engaged in an election of a school board wilfully makes or causes to be made an incorrect return of the votes given at the election, he shall, upon summary conviction, be liable to a penalty not exceeding fifty pounds; and if any person wilfully personates any person entitled to vote in the election of a school board, or answers falsely any question put to him in voting, or falsely assumes to act in the name or on the behalf of any person so entitled to vote, he shall be liable, on summary conviction, to a penalty not exceeding twenty pounds; and if any person knowingly personate and falsely assume to vote in the name of any person entitled to vote in any election, or forge or in any way falsify any name or writing in any paper purporting to contain the vote or votes of any person voting in any such election, or attempt to obstruct or prevent the purposes of any such election, or wilfully contravene any regulation made with respect to the election, the contravention of which is expressed to involve a penalty, the person so offending shall upon summary conviction be liable to a penalty of not more than fifty pounds, and in default of payment thereof to be imprisoned for a term not exceeding six months; and any person who at the election of any member of a school board or any officer appointed for the purpose of such election is guilty of corrupt practices, shall be liable to a penalty not exceeding two pounds, and be disqualified for the term of six years after such election from exercising any franchise at any election under the Act, or at any municipal or parliamentary election.

In the case of the borough of Oxford, the provisions of the Act relating to boroughs shall be construed as if the local board were therein mentioned instead of the council; if a school board is formed in the borough of Oxford, one-third of the school board shall be elected by the university of Oxford, or the colleges and halls therein, in such manner as may be directed by the education department.

After the 31st March, 1871, no parliamentary grant shall be made to any elementary school which is not a public elementary school, and no such grant shall be made in aid of building, enlarging, improving, or fitting up any elementary school, except in pursuance of a memorial duly signed, and containing the information required by the education department for enabling them to decide on the application, and sent to the department on or before the 31st December, 1870.

The conditions required to be fulfilled by an elementary school in order to obtain an annual parliamentary grant shall be those contained in the minutes of the education department in force for the time being, and shall amongst other matters provide that after the 31st March, 1871—(1.) Such grant shall not be made in respect of any instruction in religious subjects;—(2.) Such grant shall not for any year exceed the income of the school for that year which was derived from voluntary contributions, and from school fees, and from any sources other than the parliamentary grant; but such conditions shall not require that the school shall be in connexion with a religious denomination, or that religious instruction shall be given in the school, and shall not give any preference or advantage to any school on the ground that it is or is not provided by a school board.

Where the school board satisfy the education department that in any year ending 29th of September the sum required for the purpose of the annual expenses of the school board of any school district, and actually paid to the treasurer of such board by the rating authority, amounted to a sum which would have been raised by a rate of threepence in the pound on the rateable value of such district, and any such rate would have produced less than 20*l.* or less than 7*s.* 6*d.* per child of the number of children in average attendance at the public elementary schools provided by such school board, such school board shall be entitled, in addition to the annual parliamentary grant in aid of the public elementary schools provided by them, to such further sum out of moneys provided by parliament as, when added to the sum actually so paid by the rating authority, would, as the case may be, make up the sum of 20*l.*, or the sum of 7*s.* 6*d.* for each child, but no attendance shall be reckoned for the purpose of calculating such average attendance unless it is an attendance as defined in the said minutes.

Finally, the education department shall in every year cause to be laid before both Houses of Parliament a report of their proceedings under the Act during the preceding year.

THE ELEMENTARY EDUCATION ACT, 1870.

---

33 & 34 VICT. CHAP. 75.

An Act to provide for Public Elementary Education in England and Wales.

[9th August, 1870.]

BE it enacted by the Queen's most excellent Majesty, by and with the advice and consent of the Lords spiritual and temporal, and Commons, in this present Parliament assembled, and by the authority of the same, as follows; (that is to say,)

Preliminary.

1. This Act may be cited as "The Elementary Education Act, 1870." Short title

2. This Act shall not extend to Scotland or Ireland. Extent of Act.

3. In this Act—

The term "metropolis" means the places for the time being within the jurisdiction of the Definition of terms.

metropolitan board of works under the Metropolis Management Act, 1855:

A table of the parishes and places within the jurisdiction of the metropolitan board of works will be found in the Appendix, *post.*

The divisions mentioned in the fifth schedule to this Act are the parliamentary divisions of the metropolis for the purpose of the election of members of parliament. The division of which each parish forms part is shown in the table; but it will be seen that the parishes and places named embrace a larger area than the parliamentary divisions. This, however, will be rectified, as by s. 37 (2), *post*, the education department as soon as may be after the passing of this Act shall by order determine the boundaries of the divisions for the purposes of the Act.

The table also contains the population according to the census of 1861, and the rateable value of each parish as last ascertained; as to which, see sect. 39, *post.*

The term "borough" means any place for the time being subject to the Act of the session of the fifth and sixth years of the reign of King William the Fourth, chapter seventy-six, intituled "An Act to provide for the regulation of Municipal Corporations in England and Wales," and the Acts amending the same:

Schedules (A.) and (B.) of the 5 & 6 Will. 4, c. 76, contain the names of the municipal boroughs subject to the Act. But since that Act many new boroughs have been created under it by charter.

The term "parish" means a place for which for the time being a separate poor rate is or can be made:

The definition of the word "parish," in 29 & 30 Vict. c. 113, s. 18, is "a place for which a separate poor rate is or can be made, or for which a separate overseer is or can be appointed." Of course neither definition applies to an ecclesiastical istrict.

The term "person" includes a body corporate:

The term "education department" means "the lords of the committee of the privy council on education:"

The term "Her Majesty's inspectors" means the inspectors of schools appointed by Her Majesty on the recommendation of the education department:

This definition will not include inspectors of workhouse schools who are appointed by the Poor Law Board.

The term "managers" includes all persons who have the management of any elementary school, whether the legal interest in the schoolhouse is or is not vested in them:

Further, with regard to "managers," see sections 15, 21, 23 and 24, *post*.

The term "teacher" includes assistant teacher, pupil teacher, sewing mistress, and every person who forms part of the educational staff of a school:

The term "parent" includes guardian and every person who is liable to maintain or has the actual custody of any child:

This definition of the word "parent" will include "the father and grandfather, and the mother and grandmother," of any child, see 43 Eliz. c. 2. s. 7.

The term "elementary school" means a school or department of a school at which elementary education is the principal part of the education there given, and does not include any school or department of a school at which the ordinary payments in respect of the instruction, from each scholar, exceed ninepence a week:

In elementary schools, the children attend from the homes of their parents, and charge is taken of them during the school hours only.

The term "schoolhouse" includes the teacher's dwelling house, and the playground (if any) and the offices and all premises belonging to or required for a school:

The term "vestry" means the ratepayers of a parish meeting in vestry according to law:

That is, every inhabitant who shall by the last rate which shall have been made for the relief of the poor have been assessed and charged upon in respect of any annual rent, profit, or value (58 Geo. 3, c. 69, s. 3), and who shall not have refused or neglected to pay any such rate which shall be due from and shall have been demanded of him (58 Geo. 3, c. 69, s. 5), except such rates which shall have been made or become due within three calendar months immediately preceding the vestry meeting (16 & 17 Vict. c. 65, s. 1).

The term "ratepayer" includes every person who, under the provisions of the Poor Rate Assessment and Collection Act, 1869, is deemed to be duly rated:

This is an unfortunate definition of the word "ratepayer." The Act referred to does not "deem" persons to be "duly rated." Under the 43 Eliz. c. 2, s. 1, occupiers are to be rated; and under the Poor Rate Assessment and Collection Act, 1869, when sect. 4 of that Act has been adopted by the vestry of the parish, the owners of hereditaments not exceeding a certain annual rateable value are to be rated in lieu of the occupiers of such hereditaments, and in such case the franchise of the occupier, which, as regards rating, depends upon the payment of the poor rate is preserved to such occupier; but the occupier in such case is not by the Act "deemed to be duly rated." Then it is by no means clear that the owners who are rated in lieu of the occupiers are entitled to vote in vestry, seeing that sect. 6 of the Small Tenements Rating Act (13 & 14 Vict. c. 99), is not re-enacted in the Poor Rate Assessment and Collection Act, 1869.

The term "ratepayer," will of course include females who are "duly rated" under the Vestries Act, 58 Geo. 3, c. 69; they as well as males are entitled to vote in vestry.

The term "parliamentary grant" means a grant made in aid of an elementary school, either annually or otherwise, out of monies provided by parliament for the civil service, intituled "For Public Education in Great Britain."

(I.) Local Provision for Schools.

4. For the purposes of this Act the respective districts, boards, rates and funds, and authorities described in the first schedule to this Act shall be the school district, the school board, the local rate, and the rating authority. School districts, &c. in schedule.

Supply of Schools.

5. There shall be provided for every school district a sufficient amount of accommodation in public elementary schools (as hereinafter defined) available for all the children resident in such district for whose elementary education efficient and suitable provision is not otherwise made, and where there is an insufficient amount of such accommodation, in this Act referred to as "public school accommodation," the deficiency shall be supplied in manner provided by this Act. School district to have sufficient public schools.

The school districts are
1. The metropolis, according to the 18 & 19 Vict. c. 120, schedules (A.), (B.), and (C.)
2. Boroughs under the Municipal Corporations Act, 5 & 6 Will. 4, c. 76, except Oxford.
3. The district of the local board of health of Oxford.
4. Parishes for which a separate poor rate is or can be made.

See the section 7, *post*, which defines what public elementary schools shall be.

6. Where the education department, in the manner provided by this Act, are satisfied and have given public notice that there is an insufficient amount of public school accommodation for any school district, and the deficiency is not supplied as hereinafter required, a school board shall be formed Supply of schools in case of deficiency.

for such district and shall supply such deficiency, and in case of default by the school board the education department shall cause the duty of such board to be performed in manner provided by this Act

See sections 8 and 9, *post*, as to the action of the education department, and section 9 as to the supply of a deficiency of school accommodation without the intervention of a school board.

As to the action of the education department when a school board is in default, see sections 63–66, *post*.

Regulations for conduct of public elementary school.

7. Every elementary school which is conducted in accordance with the following regulations shall be a public elementary school within the meaning of this Act; and every public elementary school shall be conducted in accordance with the following regulations (a copy of which regulations shall be conspicuously put up in every such school); namely,

(1.) It shall not be required, as a condition of any child being admitted into or continuing in the school, that he shall attend or abstain from attending any Sunday school, or any place of religious worship, or that he shall attend any religious observance or any instruction in religious subjects in the school or elsewhere, from which observance or instruction he may be withdrawn by his parent, or that he shall, if withdrawn by his parent, attend the school on any day exclusively set apart for religious observance by the religious body to which his parent belongs:

See section 14, and s. 74 (2) *post*, as to religious education.

(2.) The time or times during which any religious observance is practised or instruction in religious subjects is given at any meeting of the school shall be either at the beginning or at the end or at the beginning and the end of such meeting, and shall be inserted in a time table to be approved by the education department, and to be kept permanently and conspicuously affixed in every schoolroom; and any scholar may be withdrawn by his parent from such observance or instruction without forfeiting any of the other benefits of the school:

See also section 14, and s. 74, *post*, as to religious education.

(3.) The school shall be open at all times to the inspection of any of Her Majesty's inspectors, so, however, that it shall be no part of the duties of such inspector to inquire into any instruction in religious subjects given at such school, or to examine any scholar therein in religious knowledge or in any religious subject or book:

(4.) The school shall be conducted in accordance with the conditions required to be fulfilled by an elementary school in order to obtain an annual parliamentary grant:

Proceedings for Supply of Schools.

Determination by education department of deficiency of public school accommodation.

8. For the purpose of determining with respect to every school district the amount of public school accommodation, if any, required for such district, the education department shall, immediately after the passing of this Act, cause such returns to be made as in this Act mentioned, and on receiving those returns, and after such inquiry, if any, as they think necessary, shall consider whether any and what public school accommodation is required for such district, and in so doing they shall take into consideration every school, whether public elementary or not, and whether actually situated in the school district

or not, which in their opinion gives, or will when completed give, efficient elementary education to, and is, or will when completed be, suitable for the children of such district.

See sections 67–72, *post*, as to returns.

Notice by education department of public school accommodation required.

9. The education department shall publish a notice of their decision as to the public school accommodation for any school district, setting forth with respect to such district the description thereof, the number, size, and description of the schools (if any) available for such district, which the education department have taken into consideration as above mentioned, and the amount and description of the public school accommodation, if any, which appears to them to be required for the district, and any other particulars which the education department think expedient.

If any persons being either—

(1.) Ratepayers of the district, not less than ten, or if less than ten being rated to the poor rate upon a rateable value of not less than one-third of the whole rateable valne of the district, or,

(2.) The managers of any elementary school in the district,

feel aggrieved by such decision, such persons may, within one month after the publication of the notice, apply in writing to the education department for and the education department shall direct the holding of a public inquiry in manner provided by this Act.

See note, *ante*, p. 4, as to the word "ratepayers."
As in section 73, *post*, as to public inquiries.

At any time after the expiration of such month, if no public inquiry is directed, or after the receipt of the report made after such inquiry, as the case may be, the education department may, if they think that the amount of public school accommodation for the district is insufficient, publish a final notice stating the same particulars as were contained in the former notice, with such modifications (if any) as they think fit to make, and directing that the public school accommodation therein mentioned as required be supplied.

The Act does not indicate who is to supply the public school accommodation on the direction of the education department. It seems that the department is to give a direction that it be supplied, and if the direction be not complied with by some one or other, that the school board shall be formed.

Section 41, *post*, provides for uniting school districts.

Formation of school board and requisition to provide schools.

10. If after the expiration of a time, not exceeding six months, to be limited by the final notice, the education department are satisfied that all the public school accommodation required by the final notice to be supplied has not been so supplied, nor is in course of being supplied with due despatch, the education department shall cause a school board to be formed for the district as provided in this Act, and shall send a requisition to the school board so formed requiring them to take proceedings forthwith for supplying the public school accommodation mentioned in the requisition, and the school board shall supply the same accordingly.

See section 29, *et seq.*, *post*, as to the constitution of school boards.

Proceedings on default of school board

11. If the school board fail to comply with the requisition within twelve months after the sending of such requisition in manner aforesaid, they shall be deemed to be in default, and if the education department are satisfied that such board are in default they may proceed in manner directed by this Act with respect to a school board in default.

See sections 63-66, *post*, as to defaulting school boards.

Formation of school boards without inquiry upon application.

12. In the following cases, (that is to say,)

(1.) Where application is made to the education department with respect to any school district by the persons who, if there were a school board in that district, would elect the school board, or with respect to any borough, by the council;

(2.) Where the education department are satisfied that the managers of any elementary school in any school district are unable or unwilling any longer to maintain such school, and that if the school is discontinued the amount of public school accommodation for such district will be insufficient,

the education department may, if they think fit, without making the inquiry or publishing the notices required by this Act before the formation of a school board, but after such inquiry public or other, and such notice as the education department think sufficient, cause a school board to be formed for such district, and send a requisition to such school board in the same manner in all respects as if they had published a final notice.

An application for the purposes of this section may be made by a resolution passed by the said electing body after notice published at least a week previously, or by the council, and the provisions of the second part of the second schedule to this Act with respect to the passing of such resolution shall be observed.

See section 29, *et seq.*, *post*, as to the constitution of school boards, and also section 93, as to Oxford.

See section 9, *ante*, as to inquiries by the education department, and as to the publication of a final notice, see the same section.

Proceedings by education department after the first year.

13. After the receipt of any returns under this Act subsequently to the first with respect to any school district, and after such inquiry as the educa-

tion department think necessary, the education department shall consider whether any and what public school accommodation is required in such district in the same manner as in the case of the first returns under this Act, and where in such district there is no school board acting under this Act they may issue notices and take proceedings in the same manner as they may after the receipt of the first returns under this Act, and where there is a school board in such district they shall proceed in manner directed by this Act.

As to returns under the Act, see section 8, *ante*, and see section 9, *ante*, as to public school accommodation. This section enables the education department from time to time to review the school accommodation required for any district.

Management and Maintenance of Schools by School Board.

14. Every school provided by a school board shall be conducted under the control and management of such board in accordance with the following regulations: **Management of school by school board.**

(1.) The school shall be a public elementary school within the meaning of this Act:

See the definition of "elementary schools," *ante*, p. 3, and also section 7, *ante*.

(2.) No religious catechism or religious formulary which is distinctive of any particular denomination shall be taught in the school.

See section 74 (2) as to the withdrawal of children from attendance on any religious observance or instruction in religious subjects.

15. The school board may, if they think fit, from time to time delegate any of their powers under this Act except the power of raising money, and in particular may delegate the control and **Appointment of managers by school board.**

management of any school provided by them, with or without any conditions or restrictions, to a body of managers appointed by them, consisting of not less than three persons.

The school board may from time to time remove all or any of such managers and within the limits allowed by this section add to or diminish the number of or otherwise alter the constitution or powers of any body of managers formed by it under this section.

Any manager appointed under this section may resign on giving written notice to the board. The rules contained in the third schedule to this Act respecting the proceedings of bodies of managers appointed by a school board shall be observed.

Neglect by board of regulations of public elementary schools.

16. If the school board do or permit any act in contravention of or fail to comply with the regulations according to which a school provided by them is required by this Act to be conducted, the education department may declare the school board to be and such board shall accordingly be deemed to be a board in default, and the education department may proceed accordingly, and every act or omission of any member of the school board, or manager appointed by them, or any person under the control of the board, shall be deemed to be permitted by the board, unless the contrary be proved.

If any dispute arises as to whether the school board have done or permitted any act in contravention of or have failed to comply with the said regulations, the matter shall be referred to the education department, whose decision thereon shall be final,

As to school boards in default, see sections 63-66, *post*.

This section, it will be seen, practically confers upon the education department supreme authority with regard to elementary schools which cannot be questioned, seeing that there is no appeal from the decision of the department.

Fees of children.

17. Every child attending a school provided by any school board shall pay such weekly fee as may

be prescribed by the school board, with the consent of the education department, but the school board may from time to time, for a renewable period not exceeding six months, remit the whole or any part of such fee in the case of any child when they are of opinion that the parent of such child is unable from poverty to pay the same, but such remission shall not be deemed to be parochial relief given to such parent.

See section 74 (3), *post*, as to bye laws in respect of the remission of school fees.

The 2 Will. 4, c. 45, s. 36, disqualifies persons in the receipt of parochial relief from being registered as voters for any city or borough; and by 30 & 31 Vict. c. 102, s. 40, the same disqualification applies to counties also. Hence the provision in the latter part of this section, which is similar to that in the 30 & 31 Vict. c. 84, s. 26, with regard to vaccination, at the cost of the poor rates.

Relief is now for the most part *union* and not parochial relief.

Maintenance by school board of schools and sufficient school accommodation.

18. The school board shall maintain and keep efficient every school provided by such board, and shall from time to time provide such additional school accommodation as is, in their opinion, necessary in order to supply a sufficient amount of public school accommodation for their district.

A school board may discontinue any school provided by them, or change the site of any such school, if they satisfy the education department that the school to be discontinued is unnecessary, or that such change of site is expedient.

If at any time the education department are satisfied that a school board have failed to perform their duty, either by not maintaining or keeping efficient every school provided by them, or by not providing such additional school accommodation as in the opinion of the education department is necessary in order to supply a sufficient amount of public school accommodation in their district, the education department may send them a requisition requiring them to fulfil the duty which they have so failed to perform; and if the school board fail within the time limited by such requisition, not being less than three months, to comply therewith to the satisfaction of the education department, such board shall be deemed to be a school board in default, and the education department may proceed accordingly.

See sections 63-66, *post*, as to school boards in default.

Powers of school board for providing schools.

19. Every school board for the purpose of providing sufficient public school accommodation for their district, whether in obedience to any requisition or not, may provide, by building or otherwise, schoolhouses properly fitted up, and improve, enlarge, and fit up any schoolhouse provided by them, and supply school apparatus and everything necessary for the efficiency of the schools provided by them, and purchase and take on lease any land, and any right over land, or may exercise any of such powers.

By reference to section 96, *post*, it will be seen that no application for parliamentary grants in aid of building elementary schools can be received after 31st December, 1870.

Compulsory purchase of sites.

20. With respect to the purchase of land by school boards for the purposes of this Act the following provisions shall have effect; (that is to say,)

Regulations as to the purchase of land compulsorily.

(1.) The Lands Clauses Consolidation Act, 1845, and the Acts amending the same, shall be incorporated with this Act, except the provisions relating to access to the special Act; and in construing those Acts for the purposes of this section the special Act shall be construed to mean this Act, and the promoters of the undertaking shall be construed to mean the school board, and land shall be construed to include any right over land:

The Lands Clauses Consolidation Act, 1845, and the Acts

amending the same, are the following: 8 Vict. c. 18; 23 & 24 Vict. c. 106; 32 & 33 Vict. c. 18. They will be found fully annotated, with the whole of the decisions upon them, up to the latest period, in the second volume of Shelford's Law of Railways, fourth edition, by the author of the present work.

The provision relating to access to the principal Act is contained in section 150 of the 8 Vict. c. 18, and would be inapplicable to the subject of the present Act; hence its exclusion.

The words "any right over land" would include an easement over land, such as a right of way required by the school board to obtain access to their school premises; and this they could acquire under the Act, without purchasing the land itself.

(2.) The school board, before putting in force any of the powers of the said Acts with respect to the purchase and taking of land otherwise than by agreement, shall—

As to those powers, see section 16 *et seq.*, of 8 Vict. c. 18, and the notes and cases thereon, in the second volume of Glen's Shelford on Railway Law.

Publication of notices.

(a.) Publish, during three consecutive weeks in the months of October and November, or either of them, a notice describing shortly the object for which the land is proposed to be taken, naming a place where a plan of the land proposed to be taken may be seen at all reasonable hours, and stating the quantity of land that they require; and shall further,

See section 80, *post*, as to the mode of publishing notices.

Service of notices.

(b.) After such publication, serve a notice in manner mentioned in this section on every owner or reputed owner, lessee or reputed lessee, and occupier of such land, defining in each case the particular land intended to be taken, and requiring an answer stating whether the person so served assents, dissents, or is neuter in respect of taking such land;

(c.) Such notice shall be served —

(a.) By delivery of the same personally on the person required to be served, or, if such person is absent abroad, to his agent; or

(b.) By leaving the same at the usual or last known place of abode of such person as aforesaid, or by forwarding the same by post in a registered letter, addressed to the usual or last known place of abode of such person:

Petition to education department.

(3.) Upon compliance with the provisions contained in this section with respect to notices the school board may, if they think fit, present a petition under their seal to the education department, praying that an order may be made authorizing the school board to put in force the powers of the said Acts with respect to the purchase and taking of land otherwise than by agreement, so far as regards the land therein mentioned; the petition shall state the land intended to be taken and the purposes for which it is required, and the names of the owners, lessees and occupiers of land who have assented, dissented, or are neuter in respect of the taking of such land, or who have returned no answer to the notice, and shall be supported by such evidence as the education department may from time to time require :

See section 30 (1), *post* as to the incorporation of the school board and their common seal.

(4.) If, on consideration of the petition and proof of the publication and service of the proper notices, the education department think fit to proceed with the case, they may, if they think fit, appoint some person to inquire in the district in which the land is situate respecting the propriety of the proposed order, and also direct such person to hold a public inquiry :

(5.) After such consideration and proof, and after receiving a report made upon any such inquiry, the education department may make the order prayed for, authorizing the school board to put in force with reference to the land referred to in such order the powers of the said Acts with respect to the purchase and taking of land otherwise than by agreement, or any of them, and either absolutely or with such conditions and modifications as they may think fit, and it shall be the duty of the school board to serve a copy of any order so made in the manner and upon the persons in which and upon whom notices in respect of the land to which the order relates are required by this Act to be served :

Duplicate copies of the order will doubtless be supplied by the education department for service; the copy will be served according to the previous sub-section (2), sub-division (c).

(6.) No order so made shall be of any validity unless the same has been confirmed by

No order valid until

confirmed by parliament.

Act of parliament; and it shall be lawful for the education department, as soon as conveniently may be, to obtain such confirmation, and the Act confirming such order shall be deemed to be a public general Act of parliament:

The confirmation of the order will not be obtained in the same way that the confirmation of provisional orders by parliament is obtained by the board of trade or the secretary of state, or Poor Law Board. There the bill for confirming the order is dealt with, and may be petitioned against in like manner as a private bill, and when it is passed it is classed amongst the private Acts of parliament. Here the Act is to be deemed a public general Act of parliament, and petitioners against the bill cannot be heard before a select committee as in the case of a bill for confirming a provisional order; moreover, though essentially of a local and personal nature, the Act will be classed amongst the public general Acts, thus breaking through the rule so recently established by Sir John George Shaw Lefevre, as to the classification of the statutes.

(7.) The education department, in case of their refusing or modifying such order, may make such order as they think fit for the allowance of the costs, charges, and expenses of any person whose land is proposed to be taken of and incident to such application and inquiry respectively:

Costs how to be defrayed.

(8.) All costs, charges, and expenses incurred by the education department in relation to any order under this section shall, to such amount as the commissioners of Her Majesty's treasury think proper to direct, and all costs, charges, and expenses of any person which shall be so allowed by the education department as aforesaid shall, become a charge upon the school fund of the district to which such order relates, and be repaid to the said commissioners of Her Majesty's treasury or to such person respectively, by annual instalments not exceeding five, together with interest after the yearly rate of five pounds in the hundred, to be computed from the date of any such direction of the said commissioners, or allowance of such costs, charges, and expenses respectively upon so much of the principal sum due in respect of the said costs, charges, and expenses as may from time to time remain unpaid.

The School Sites Acts as defined in the fourth schedule to this Act shall apply in the same manner as if the school board were trustees or managers of a school within the meaning of those Acts, and land may be acquired under any of the Acts mentioned in this section, or partly under one and partly under another Act.

The Acts referred to as being mentioned in the latter part of this section are the Lands Clauses Consolidation Act, 1845, and the Acts amending the same.

Purchase of land by managers of public elementary school.

21. For the purpose of the purchase by the managers of any public elementary school of a school-house for such school, or a site for the same, "The Lands Clauses Consolidation Act, 1845," and the Acts amending the same, (except so much as relates to the purchase of land otherwise than by agreement,) shall be incorporated with this Act; and in construing those Acts for the purposes of this section the special Act shall be construed to mean this Act, and the promoters of the undertaking shall be construed to mean such managers, and land shall be construed to include any right over land.

The conveyance of any land so purchased may be in the form prescribed by the School Sites Acts, or any of them, with this modification, that the conveyance shall express that the land shall be held upon trust for the purposes of a public elementary school within the meaning of this Act, or some one of such purposes which may be specified, and for no other purpose whatever.

Land may be acquired under the Acts incorporated with this section, or under the School Sites Acts, or any of them, or partly under one and partly under another Act.

Any persons desirous of establishing a public elementary school shall be deemed to be managers for the purpose of this section if they obtain the approval of the education department to the establishment of such school.

This section was introduced in the House of Lords. It will be seen that it has reference to the purchase of schools and sites by the managers of public elementary schools; section 20 has reference to the purchase of land by school boards.

As to the incorporated Lands Clauses Acts, see note to section 20 (1), *ante*.

Sale or lease of school-house.

22. The provisions of the Charitable Trusts Acts, 1853 to 1869, which relate to the sale, leasing, and exchange of lands belonging to any charity, shall extend to the sale, leasing, and exchange of the whole or any part of any land or schoolhouse belonging to a school board which may not be required by such board, with this modification, that the education department shall for the purposes of this section be deemed to be substituted in those Acts for the charity commissioners.

The provisions referred to of the Charitable Trusts Act are contained in 16 & 17 Vict. c. 137, 18 & 19 Vict. c. 124, 23 & 24 Vict. c. 136, 25 & 26 Vict. c. 112, and 32 & 33 Vict. c. 110 They will be found in the Appendix, *post*. Further, with reference to this section and those Acts, see section 78, *post*.

Managers may transfer school to school board.

23. The managers of any elementary school in the district of a school board may, in manner provided by this Act, make an arrangement with the school board for transferring their school to such school board, and the school board may assent to such arrangement.

An arrangement under this section may be made by the managers by a resolution or other act as follows; (that is to say,)

(1.) Where there is any instrument declaring the trusts of the school, and such instrument provides any manner in which or any assent with which a resolution or act binding the managers is to be passed or done, then in accordance with the provisions of such instrument:

(2.) Where there is no such instrument, or such instrument contains no such provisions, then in the manner and with the assent, if any, in and with which it may be shown to the education department to have been usual for a resolution or act binding such managers to be passed or done:

(3.) If no manner or assent can be shown to have been usual, then by a resolution passed by a majority of not less than two-thirds of those members of their body who are present at a meeting of the body summoned for the purpose, and vote on the question, and with the assent of any other person whose assent under the circumstances appears to the education department to be requisite.

And in every case such arrangement shall be made only—

(1.) With the consent of the education department; and,

(2.) If there are annual subscribers to such school, with the consent of a majority, not being less than two-thirds in number, of those of the annual subscribers who are present at a meeting duly summoned for the purpose, and vote on the question.

A question will here arise as to who is an "annual subscriber." Will one who is in arrear with one or more annual subscriptions have a right to be present and vote, or will as many as like to come forward and pay only one annual subscription have a like right? Perhaps, however, it may be found that the instrument if there be one, declaring the trusts of the school, defines who shall be deemed annual subscribers.

Provided that where there is any instrument declaring the trusts of the school, and such instrument contains any provision for the alienation of the school by any persons or in any manner or subject to any consent, any arrangement under this section shall be made by the persons in the manner and with the consent so provided.

Where it appears to the education department that there is any trustee of the school who is not a manager, they shall cause the managers to serve on such trustee, if his name and address are known, such notice as the education department think sufficient; and the education department shall consider and have due regard to any objections and representations he may make respecting the proposed transfer.

The education department shall consider and have due regard to any objections and representations respecting the proposed transfer which may be made by any person who has contributed to the establishment of such school.

After the expiration of six months from the date of transfer the consent of the education department shall be conclusive evidence that the arrangement has been made in conformity with this section.

An arrangement under this section may provide for the absolute conveyance to the school board of all the interest in the schoolhouse possessed by the managers or by any person who is trustee for them or for the school, or for the lease of the same, with or without any restrictions, and either at a nominal rent or otherwise, to the school board, or for the use by the school board of the schoolhouse during part of the week, and for the use of the same by the managers or some other person during the remainder of the week, or for any arrangement that may be agreed on. The arrangement may also provide for the transfer or application of any endowment belonging to the school, or for the school board undertaking to discharge any debt charged on the school not exceeding the value of the interest in the schoolhouse or endowment transferred to them.

When an arrangement is made under this section the managers may, whether the legal interest in the schoolhouse or endowment is vested in them or in some person as trustee for them or the school, convey to the school board all such interest in the schoolhouse and endowment as is vested in them or in such trustee, or such smaller interest as may be required under the arrangement.

Nothing in this section shall authorize the managers to transfer any property which is not vested in them, or a trustee for them, or held in trust for the school; and where any person has any right given him by the trusts of the school to use the school for any particular purpose independently of such managers, nothing in this section shall authorize any interference with such right except with the consent of such person.

Every school so transferred shall, to such extent and during such times as the school board have under such arrangement any control over the school, be deemed to be a school provided by the school board.

24. Where any school or any interest therein has been transferred by the managers thereof to the school board of any school district in pursuance of this Act, the school board of such district may, by a resolution passed as hereinafter mentioned, and with the consent of the education department, re- **Retransfer of school by school board to managers.**

transfer such school or such interest therein to a body of managers qualified to hold the same under the trusts of the school as they existed before such transfer to the school board, and upon such re-transfer may convey all the interest in the school-house and in any endowment belonging to the school vested in the school board.

A resolution for the purpose of this section may be passed by a majority of not less than two-thirds of those members of the school board who are present at a meeting duly convened for the purpose, and vote on the question.

The education department shall not give their consent to any such re-transfer unless they are satisfied that any money expended upon such school out of a loan raised by the school board of such district has been or will on the completion of the re-transfer be repaid to the school board.

Every school so re-transferred shall cease to be a school provided by a school board, and shall be held upon the same trusts on which it was held before it was transferred to the school board.

As to the borrowing powers of the school board, see ss. 57 and 58, *post.*

This clause was introduced in the House of Lords. Section 76, *post,* provides for the inspection of voluntary schools.

Miscellaneous Powers of School Board.

Payment of school fees.

25. The school board may, if they think fit, from time to time, for a renewable period not exceeding six months, pay the whole or any part of the school fees payable at any public elementary school by any child resident in their district whose parent is in their opinion unable from poverty to pay the same; but no such payment shall be made or refused on condition of the child attending any public ele-

mentary school other than such as may be selected by the parent; and such payment shall not be deemed to be parochial relief given to such parent.

See note to s. 17, *ante*, p. 13, as to parochial relief.

26. If a school board satisfy the education department that, on the ground of the poverty of the inhabitants of any place in their district, it is expedient for the interests of education to provide a school at which no fees shall be required from the scholars, the board may, subject to such rules and conditions as the education department may prescribe, provide such school, and may admit scholars to such school without requiring any fee. Establishment of free school in special cases.

"The poverty of the inhabitants" contemplated is the poverty of those inhabitants whose children are likely to attend the elementary school. It may be that there are many wealthy inhabitants, but that nevertheless the poverty of the others may require that a free school shall be provided at which their children may attend. The word "place" is mentioned, and this means any particular locality in the district of the school board in which the very poor do congregate.

27. A school board shall have the same powers of contributing money in the case of an industrial school as is given to a prison authority by section twelve of "The Industrial Schools Act, 1866;" and upon the election of a school board in a borough the council of that borough shall cease to have power to contribute under that section. Contribution to industrial schools. 29 & 30 Vict. c. 118.

Section 12 of the Industrial Schools Act, 1866 (29 & 30 Vict. c. 118) is as follows:—"In England a prison authority may from time to time contribute such sums of money, and on such conditions as they think fit, towards the alteration, enlargement, or rebuilding of a certified industrial school, or towards the support of the inmates of such a school, or towards the management of such a school, or towards the establishment or building of a school intended to be a certified industrial school, or towards the purchase of land required either for the use of an existing certified industrial school, or for the site of a school intended to be a certified industrial school; provided,—

First, that not less than two months previous notice of the intention of the prison authority to take into consideration the making of such contribution, at a time and place to be mentioned in such notice, be given by advertiscment in some one or more public newspaper or newspapers circulated within the district of the county or borough, and also in the manner in which notices relating to business to be transacted by the prison authority are usually given.

Secondly, that where the prison authority is the council of a borough, the order for the contribution be made at a special meeting of the council.

Thirdly, that where the contribution is for alteration, enlargement, rebuilding, establishment, or building of a school or intended school, or for purchase of land, the approval of the secretary of state be previously given for that alteration, enlargement, rebuilding, establishment, building, or purchase.

Section 13 of the Industrial Schools Act provides for the mode of obtaining the approval of the secrctary of state as last mentioned; but looking to section 28 of the present Act, the consent of the education department would seem to be all that is requisite in the case of a school board acting under section 12.

Establishment of industrial school.

28. A school board may, with the consent of the education department, establish, build, and maintain a certified industrial school within the meaning of the Industrial Schools Act, 1866, and shall for that purpose have the same powers as they have for the purpose of providing sufficient school accommodation for their district: provided that the school board, so far as regards any such industrial school, shall be subject to the jurisdiction of one of Her Majesty's principal secretaries of state in the same manner as the managers of any other industrial school are subject, and such school shall be subject to the provisions of the said Act, and not of this Act.

Section 5 of the 29 & 30 Vict. c. 118, describes an industrial school and the managers thereof, as follows:—"A school in which industrial training is provided, and in which children are lodged, clothed, and fed, as well as taught, shall exclusively be deemed an industrial school within the meaning of this Act.

"The persons for the time being having the management or control of such a school shall be deemed the managers thereof, for the purposes of this Act."

The powers of a school board for the purpose of providing sufficient school accommodation for their district are contained in sections 19, 20, and 22, *ante*.

The Industrial Schools Act, 1866, must be referred to generally for the powers and authorities of the secretary of state under it. It will be found in Glen's Poor Law Statutes, 43 Eliz. c. 2, to the present time.

Constitution of School Boards.

School board.

29. The school board shall be elected in manner provided by this Act,—in a borough by the persons whose names are on the burgess roll of such borough for the time being in force, and in a parish not situate in the metropolis by the ratepayers.

The first part of schedule 2, *post*, provides for the mode of election. As regards elections by "ratepayers," see note, *ante*, p. 4; and as to Oxford, see s. 93, *post*.

At every such election every voter shall be entitled to a number of votes equal to the number of the members of the school board to be elected, and may give all such votes to one candidate, or may distribute them among the candidates, as he thinks fit.

This is a mode of voting whereby all the votes can be given for one candidate. It has been generally abandoned in voting in charitable societies, and is quite opposed to the system of voting in vestry and in the election of guardians of the poor.

The school board in the metropolis shall be elected in manner herein-after provided by this Act.

See section 37, *post*, as to the election of the school board in the metropolis.

Constitution of school board.

30. With respect to the constitution of a school board the following provisions shall have effect:

(1.) The school board shall be a body corporate, by the name of the school board of the district to which they belong, having a perpetual succession and a common seal, with power to acquire and hold land for the purposes of this Act without any licence in mortmain.

(2.) No act or proceeding of the school board shall be questioned on account of any vacancy or vacancies in their body:

There must, nevertheless, be a quorum of members present according to the third schedule, *post*, article 1, subsection (e).

(3.) No disqualification of or defect in the election of any persons or person acting as members or member of the school board shall be deemed to vitiate any proceedings of such board in which they or he have taken part, in cases where the majority of members parties to such proceedings were duly entitled to act:

The majority of members present duly entitled to act, and parties to the proceedings must however constitute a quorum of members.

(4.) Any minute made of proceedings at meetings of the school board, if signed by any person purporting to be the chairman of the board, either at the meeting of the board at which such proceedings took place or at the next ensuing meeting of the board shall be receivable in evidence in all legal proceedings without further proof, and until the contrary is proved every meeting of the school board, in respect to the proceedings of which minutes have been so made, shall be deemed to have been duly convened and held, and all the members thereof to have been duly qualified to act:

(5.) The members of a school board may apply any money in their hands for the purpose of indemnifying themselves against any law costs or damages which they may incur in or in consequence of the execution of the powers granted to them:

Practically, therefore, the members will incur no personal responsibility in respect of the execution of their powers; but such responsibility will attach if they act *ultra vires*, that is, beyond their statutory powers. But see s. 60, subsection (6), *post*.

(6.) The rules contained in the third schedule to this Act with respect to the proceedings of school boards, and the other matters therein contained, shall be observed.

31. With respect to the election under this Act of a school board, except in the metropolis, the following provisions shall have effect: **Election of school board.**

(1.) The number of members of a school board shall be such number, not less than five nor more than fifteen, as may be determined in the first instance by the education department, and afterwards from time to time by a resolution of the school board approved by the education department.

(2.) The regulations contained in the second schedule to this Act with respect to the election and retirement of the members of the school board, and the other matters therein contained, shall be of the same force as if they were enacted as part of this section.

(3.) The education department may, at any time after the date at which they are authorised under this Act to cause a school board to be formed, send a requisition to the mayor or other officer or officers who have power to take proceedings for holding the election requiring him or them to take such proceedings, and the mayor or other officer or officers shall comply with such requisition; and in case of default some person appointed by the education department may take such proceedings, and shall have for that purpose the same powers as the person in default.

As to the formation of school boards see sect. 10, *ante.*

Non-election, &c. of school board.

32. If from any cause in any school district the school board either are not elected at the time fixed for the first election, or at any time cease to be in existence, or to be of sufficient number to form a quorum by reason of non-election, resignation or otherwise, or neglect or refuse to act, the education department may proceed in the same manner as if there were a school board acting in such district, and that board were a board in default.

As to school boards in default see sect. 63, *post.*

Determination of disputes as to the election of school boards.

33. In case any question arises as to the right of any person to act as a member of a school board under this Act, the education department may, if they think fit, inquire into the circumstances of the case, and make such order as they deem just for determining the question, and such order shall be final unless removed by writ of *certiorari* during the term next after the making of such order.

With regard to the writ of *certiorari*, see 5 & 6 W. and M. c. 11; 8 & 9 Will. 3, c. 33; 5 Geo. 2, c. 19, ss. 2, 3; 13 Geo. 2, c. 18, s. 5, and 5 & 6 Will. 4, c. 33, ss. 1, 2, in Glen's Poor Law Statutes.

But see section 84, *post*, as to the legal effect of requisitions of the education department, and also section 44.

See the correlative provision in 5 & 6 Vict. c. 57, s. 8. *Quo warranto*, it would seem, would lie notwithstanding.

34. No member of a school board, and no manager appointed by them, shall hold or accept any place of profit the appointment to which is vested in the school board or in any managers appointed by them, nor shall in any way share or be concerned in the profits of any bargain or contract with or any work done under the authority of such school board or managers appointed by them: provided that this section shall not apply to— **Disqualification of member of board.**

(1.) Any sale of land or loan of money to a school board; or,

(2.) Any bargain or contract made with or work done by a company in which such member holds shares;

(3.) The insertion of any advertisement relating to the affairs of any such school board in any newspaper in which such member has a share or interest,

if he does not vote with respect to such sale, loan, bargain, contract, work, or insertion.

Any person who acts in contravention of this section shall be liable, on summary conviction, to a penalty not exceeding fifty pounds, and the said place of profit and his office as member or manager shall be vacant.

This penal provision will be enforced summarily under Jervis's Act, 11 & 12 Vict. c. 43; see s. 92, *post*, and Glen's Jervis's Acts, third edition.

35. A school board may appoint a clerk and a treasurer and other necessary officers, including the teachers required for any school provided by such board, to hold office during the pleasure of the board, and may assign them such salaries or remuneration (if any) as they think fit, and may from time to time remove any of such officers; but no such appointment shall be made, except at the first meeting of such board, unless notice in writing has been sent to every member of the board. **Appointment of officers.**

Two or more school boards may arrange for the appointment of the same person to be an officer to both or all such boards.

Such officers shall perform such duties as may be assigned to them by the board or boards who appoint them.

It will be seen that the school board have entire control over their officers and the fixing of their salaries, and that there is no appeal given for the protection of the officer.

Officer to enforce attendance at school.

36. Every school board may, if they think fit, appoint an officer or officers to enforce any byelaws under this Act with reference to the attendance of children at school, and to bring children who are liable under the Industrial Schools Act, 1866, to be sent to a certified industrial school before two justices in order to their being so sent, and any expenses incurred under this section may be paid out of the school fund.

See section 74 as to the making of bye-laws by school boards.

The following are the provisions of the Industrial Schools Act, 1866, as to the classes of children who are liable to be detained in certified industrial schools:

14. Any person may bring before two justices or a magistrate any child apparently under the age of fourteen years that comes within any of the following descriptions, namely,—

That is found begging or receiving alms (whether actually or under the pretext of selling or offering for sale any thing), or being in any street or public place for the purpose of so begging or receiving alms;

That is found wandering and not having any home or settled place of abode, or proper guardianship, or visible means of subsistence;

That is found destitute, either being an orphan or having a surviving parent who is undergoing penal servitude or imprisonment;

That frequents the company of reputed thieves.

The justices or magistrate before whom a child is brought as coming within one of those descriptions, if satisfied on inquiry of that fact, and that it is expedient to deal with him under this Act, may order him to be sent to a certified industrial school.

15. Where a child apparently under the age of twelve years is charged before two justices or a magistrate with an offence

punishable by imprisonment or a less punishment, but has not been in England convicted of felony, or in Scotland of theft, and the child ought, in the opinion of the justices or magistrate, (regard being had to his age and to the circumstances of the case,) to be dealt with under this Act, the justices or magistrate may order him to be sent to a certified industrial school.

16. Where the parent or step-parent or guardian of a child apparently under the age of fourteen years represents to two justices or a magistrate that he is unable to control the child, and that he desires that the child be sent to an industrial school under this Act, the justices or magistrate, if satisfied on inquiry that it is expedient to deal with the child under this Act, may order him to be sent to a certified industrial school.

17. Where the guardians of the poor of a union or of a parish wherein relief is administered by a board of guardians, or the board of management of a district pauper school, or the parochial board of a parish or combination, represent to two justices or a magistrate that any child apparently under the age of fourteen years maintained in a workhouse or pauper school of a union or parish, or in a district pauper school, or in the poorshouse of a parish or combination, is refractory, or is the child of parents either of whom has been convicted of a crime or offence punishable with penal servitude or imprisonment, and that it is desirable that he be sent to an industrial school under this Act, the justices or magistrate may, if satisfied that it is expedient to deal with the child under this Act, order him to be sent to a certified industrial school.

School Board in Metropolis.

37. The provisions of this Act with respect to the formation and the election of school boards in boroughs and parishes shall not extend to the metropolis; and with respect to a school board in the metropolis the following provisions shall have effect: **Schoolboard in metropolis.**

(1.) The school board shall consist of such number of members elected by the divisions specified in the fifth schedule to this Act as the education department may by order fix:

See subsection (9) as to the chairman, who need not necessarily be an elected member, in this respect following the precedent of the chairman of the Metropolitan Board of Works.

(2.) The education department, as soon as may

be after the passing of this Act, shall by order determine the boundaries of the said divisions for the purposes of this Act, and the number of members to be elected by each such division:

See the table in the Appendix, *post*, as to the parishes and places within the jurisdiction of the metropolitan board of works.

(3.) The provisions of this Act with respect to the constitution of the school board shall extend to the constitution of the school board under this section, and the name of the school board shall be the School Board for London:

As to the Constitution of School Boards, see ss. 29 and 36, *ante*.

(4.) The first election of the school board shall take place on such day, as soon as may be after the passing of this Act, as the education department may appoint, and subsequent elections shall take place in the month of November every third year on the day from time to time appointed by the school board:

(5.) At every election for each division every voter shall be entitled to a number of votes equal to the number of the members of the school board to be elected for such division, and may give all such votes to one candidate, or may distribute them among the candidates, as he thinks fit:

The divisions are those specified in the fifth Schedule, *post*. See note to section 29, *ante*, p. 27, as to the mode of voting.

(6.) Subject to the provisions contained in this section and in any order made by the education department under the power contained in the second schedule to this Act, the members of the board shall, in the city of London, be elected by the same persons and in like manner as common councilmen are elected, and in the other divisions of the metropolis shall be elected by the same persons and in the same manner as vestrymen under The Metropolis Management Act, 1855, and the Acts amending the same; and, subject as aforesaid, the Acts relating to the election of common councilmen, and sections fourteen to nineteen, and twenty-one to twenty-seven, all inclusive, of The Metropolis Management Act, 1855, and section thirty-six of the Metropolis Management Amendment Act, 1862, shall, so far as is consistent with the tenor thereof, apply in the case of the election of members of the school board :

The statutes 12 & 13 Vict. cap. xciv, and 30 & 31 Vict. cap. i, regulate the election of common councilmen in the city of London. By the latter Act, every *male* person of full age, not subject to any legal incapacity, rated for premises to the police or any other rate at an annual value of at least £10, and every person on the register of parliamentary voters, or entitled to be on the register, is qualified to vote in the election of common councilmen in the ward in which the qualifying premises shall be situated. But the members of the school board for London are not to be elected for wards but for the whole city; and though they may be elected by the same persons it does not seem that they can be elected "in like manner as common councilmen." But it will be seen from the second schedule, Article (4), *post*, that the education department may make an order as to elections which, so far as relates to the metropolis, shall supersede any provisions contained in the Acts relating to the election of common councilmen, and in the Metropolis Management Act, 1855, and the Acts amending the same.

The several sections of the Metropolis Management Acts mentioned in this section will be found in the Appendix, *post*.

Under the Metropolis Local Management Act, "parishioners" are to elect (section 16), and the word includes females. Per Lord Hardwick, C., in Attorney-General *v.* Parker, 3 Atk. 577. "Parishioners is a very large word, taking in not only inhabitants of the parish, but persons who are occupiers of lands that pay the several rates and duties, though they are not resident, nor do contribute to the ornaments of the church." Females however it will be seen are excluded from voting in the city of London. By 32 & 33 Vict. c. 55, s. 9, they can vote in boroughs.

(7.) The school board shall proceed at once to supply their district with sufficient public school accommodation, and any requisition sent by the education department to such board may relate to any of the divisions mentioned in the fifth schedule to this Act in like manner as if it were a school district, and it shall not be necessary for the education department to publish any notices before sending such requisition:

As to publishing notices see section 9, *ante.*

(8.) The education department may, in the order fixing the boundaries of such divisions name some person who shall be the returning officer for the purposes of the first election of the school board, and the person who is to be the deputy returning officer in each such division:

(9.) The chairman of the school board shall be elected by the school board, and any chairman who may be elected by the board may be elected either from the members of the board or not, and any chairman who is not an elected member of the board shall, by virtue of his office, be a member of the board as if he had been so elected:

If the chairman be not an elected member he will be in addition to the number of elected members as fixed by the education department under subsection (1) of this section. See s. 38, *post*, as to paying a salary to the chairman.

(10.) The school board shall apportion the amount required to be raised to meet the deficiency in the school fund among the different parts of the metropolis mentioned in the third column of the first schedule to this Act in proportion to the rateable value of such parts as shown by the valuation lists for the time being in force under "The Valuation (Metropolis) Act, 1869," or, if any amount is so required before any such valuation list comes into force, in the same proportion and according to the same basis in and according to which the then last rate made by the metropolitan board of works was assessed:

By section 79, *post*, the persons having the custody of valuation lists and rate books shall, when required by the school board, produce such lists and rate books to them, and allow the same to be inspected, or copies of them, or extracts from them to be made.

(11.) For obtaining payment of the amount specified in any precept sent by the school board to the rating authority for any part of the metropolis, the school board, in addition to any other powers and remedies, shall have the like powers as the metropolitan board of works have for obtaining payment of any sum assessed by them on the same part of the metropolis.

See 18 & 19 Vict. c. 120, ss. 172, 173 and 174; and 25 & 26 Vict. c. 102, ss. 12, 13 in the Appendix to this work, as to the powers of the Metropolitan Board of Works in this respect.

Payment of chairman.

38. The school board for London may pay to the chairman of such board such salary as they may from time to time, with the sanction of the education department, fix.

Alteration of number of members.

39. If at any time application is made to the education department by the school board for London, or by any six members of that board, and it is shown to the satisfaction of the education department that the population of any of the divi-

sions mentioned in the fifth schedule to this Act, as shown by any census taken under the authority of parliament, has varied materially from that shown by the previous census, or that the rateable value of any of the said divisions has materially varied from the rateable value of the same division ten years previously, the education department, after such inquiry as they think necessary, may, if they think fit, make an order altering, by way of increase or decrease, the number of members of that and any other division.

In the Appendix, *post*, will be found a table of the parishes and places within the metropolis, distinguishing the division (parliamentary) in which each is situated; and containing also the population and annual rateable value of each place.

As to the proceedings which are to take place should the number of members be reduced, see the first part of the second schedule, article 18, *post*.

United School Districts.

Formation by education department of united districts.

40. Where the education department are of opinion that it would be expedient to form a school district larger than a borough or a parish or any school district formed under this Act, they may, except in the metropolis, by order made after such inquiry and notice as herein-after mentioned, form a united school district by uniting any two or more adjoining school districts, and upon such union cause a school board to be formed for such united school district.

A united school district shall for all the purposes of this Act be deemed to be a school district, and shall throughout this Act be deemed to be substituted for the school districts out of which it is constituted, and the school board of the united school district shall be the school board appointed under this Act, and the local rate and rating authority for the united district shall be in each of the constituent districts thereof the same as if such constituent district did not form part of the united school district.

As to the notice and inquiry referred to in this section, see section 41, *post*.

If part of the united school district be a borough, the council of the borough shall be the rating authority for that part; and if the other part be a parish, the overseers shall be the rating authority for that part. If two or more parishes, then the overseers of each parish shall be the rating authority.

Conditions of formation of district.

41. The education department, as soon as may be after the passing of this Act, may cause inquiry to be made into the expediency of uniting any two or more school districts, and if after such inquiry they are of opinion that it would be expedient to unite any such school districts, they shall in the notice of their decision as to the public school accommodation for such districts state that they propose to unite such districts, and the provisions of this Act with respect to the application for a public inquiry by persons aggrieved by the said notice, and to the holding of such public inquiry, and to the final notice, shall apply in the case of the proposed union of districts, with this qualification, that it shall not be necessary to cause a public inquiry to be held with respect to the union of districts until after the expiration of the period allowed by the final notice for the supply of the school accommodation. The order for the union may be made at the time when the education department are first authorized to cause a school board to be formed or subsequently. Where a union of districts is proposed the education department shall consider whether any public school accommodation is required for the area proposed as the united district instead of for each of the districts constituting such area, and their decision as to the public school accommodation and the notice of such decision shall accordingly refer to such area, and not separately to each of the constituent districts.

See section 9, *ante*, p. 8, as to the notice of the education department as to the school accommodation required.

Section 9, *ante*, p. 8, and section 73, *post*, provides for the holding of the public inquiry referred to in this section.

As to dissolution of united school district.

42. The education department may, by order made after such inquiry and notice as herein-after mentioned, dissolve a united school district, and may deal with the constituent districts thereof in the same manner as if they had never been united, and may cause school boards to be elected therein.

The notice hereinafter mentioned is that in section 43, *infra*, as to the formation of school boards.
See sections 9—12, *ante*.

Public inquiry as to united district in future.

43. The education department may at any time, after any proceedings after the first returns under this Act, if they think fit, cause inquiry to be made into the expediency of forming or dissolving a united school district, and where they propose at any time after such inquiry to form or dissolve a united school district, they shall publish notice of the proposed order not less than three months before the order is made; the like persons as are authorized to apply for a public inquiry after the first returns made under this Act may, if they feel aggrieved by the proposed order, apply in like manner for a public inquiry, and the education department shall cause a public inquiry to be held, and shall consider the report made to them upon such inquiry before they make the order for such formation or dissolution.

See section 8, *ante*, p. 7, as to the first returns under the Act, and section 80, *post*, as to the mode of publication of notices.
As to an application for a public inquiry see section 9, (1) and (2), *ante*.

Order to be evidence of formation or dissolution.

44. Any order of the education department forming or dissolving a united district shall be evidence of the formation or dissolution of such district, and after the expiration of three months from the date of such order the district shall be presumed to have been duly formed or dissolved, as

the case may be, and no objection to the formation or dissolution thereof shall be entertained in any legal proceedings whatever.

The writ of *certiorari* is not taken away by the Act; and therefore within the three months the order fixing or dissolving the united district may be removed into the Court of Queen's Bench for the purpose of being quashed.
As to the writ of *certiorari*, see section 33, *ante*, p. 30.

Constitution of school board in united school district.

45. The provisions in this Act respecting the constitution of the school board shall apply to the constitution of the school board in a united school district, and the name of the district shall be such as may be prescribed by the education department.

See sections 29—36, *ante*, as to the constitution of school boards.

Election of school board in united school district.

46. In a united school district the school board shall be such number of members elected by the electors of the district as may be specified in the order forming the district, subject nevertheless to alteration in the same manner as in the case of any other school board; and every person who in any of the districts constituting such united district would be entitled if it were not united to vote at the election of members of a school board for such constituent district shall be an elector for the purposes of this section, and the provisions of this Act respecting the election of a school board in a district shall extend to the election of such members.

As to the alteration of the number of members constituting a school board, see s. 31, (1), *ante*, p. 29.
See sect. 29, *ante*, p. 27, and the first part of the second schedule of this Act as to the election of members. In a united district the electors of each constituent part will be entitled to vote for all or any of the members proposed for election for the united district.

Arrangements on formation of united district.

47. Where any part of a proposed united school district includes any district or part of a district in which there is a school board already acting under

this Act, or where a united school district is dissolved, the education department may by order dissolve the then existing school board, or make all necessary changes in the constitution of such existing school board, and may by order make proper arrangements respecting the schools, property, rights, and liabilities of such board, and all arrangements which may be necessary.

The arrangements to be made under this section will be in the absolute discretion of the education department. But where real property has been acquired by the school board (see ss. 19, 20, *ante*), some difficulty may arise in regard thereto if a united district be dissolved.

As to small parishes.

48. If the education department are of opinion that any parish in a united school district has too few ratepayers to be entitled to act as a separate parish for the purposes of this Act, they may by order direct that it shall for the purpose of voting for a member or members of the school board, and for all or any of the purposes of this Act, be added to another parish, and thereupon the persons who would be entitled to vote and attend the vestry if it were a parish shall be entitled for the purpose of voting and for such purposes to vote in and attend the vestry of the parish to which their parish is so added. All the parishes comprised in a united district, or any two or more of them, may be added together in pursuance of this section.

The ratepayers (as to whom, see *ante*, p. 4), of the smaller parish must, under this section, attend the vestry of the larger parish. They will not meet for the purposes of the Act in their own vestry

Contributory Districts.

Contributory district.

49. The education department my by order direct that one school district shall contribute towards the provision or maintenance of public elementary schools in another school district or districts, and in

such case the former (or contributing district) shall pay to the latter (or school owning district or districts) such proportion of the expenses of such provision or maintenance or a sum calculated in such manner as the education department may from time to time prescribe.

50. Where one school district contributes to the provision or maintenance of any school in another school district, such number of persons as the education department (having regard to the amount to be contributed by the contributing district) direct shall be elected in the contributing district, and shall be members of the school board of the school owning district, but such last-mentioned district shall, except so far as regards the raising of money and the attendance of children at school, be deemed alone to be the district of such school board; such members shall be elected by the school board, if any, or, if there is none, by the persons who would elect a school board if there were one, in the same manner as a school board would be elected.

Election of members by contributory district.

51. The provisions of this Act with respect to the notices to be published, and the application for and the holding of a public inquiry in the case of an order for the formation of an united district, shall apply *mutatis mutandis,* to an order respecting a contributory district.

Notices and public inquiry as to contributory district.

An order respecting a contributory district shall be evidence of the formation of such district, and after the expiration of three months from the date thereof shall be presumed to have been duly made, and no objection to the legality thereof shall be entertained in any legal proceeding whatever.

Any such order may be revoked or altered by an order of the education department, and a new order may be made in lieu thereof, and all the provisions of this Act respecting the making of an order for contribution shall apply to the making of an order for the revocation or alteration of an order for contribution.

See ss. 9 and 41, *ante*, and s. 73, *post*, with regard to the provision in this section.

See s. 44, *ante*, p. 40, and note thereon as to evidence of the formation or dissolution of a school district.

Combination of school boards.

52. The school boards of any two or more school districts, with the sanction of the education department, may combine together for any purpose relating to elementary schools in such districts, and in particular may combine for the purpose of providing, maintaining, and keeping efficient schools common to such districts. Such agreements may provide for the appointment of a joint body of managers under the provisions of this Act with respect to the appointment of a body of managers, and for the proportion of the contributions to be paid by each school district, and any other matters which, in the opinion of the education department, are necessary for carrying out such agreement, and the expenses of such joint body of managers shall be paid in the proportions specified in the agreement by each of the school boards out of their school fund.

See s. 15, *ante*, p. 11, as to the appointment of managers of school boards.

Expenses.

School fund of school board.

53. The expenses of the school board under this Act shall be paid out of a fund called the school fund. There shall be carried to the school fund all moneys received as fees from scholars, or out of moneys provided by parliament, or raised by way of loan, or in any manner whatever received by the school board, and any deficiency shall be raised by the school board as provided by this Act.

See ss. 17, 25 and 26, *ante*, as to school fees.

As to the conditions on which parliamentary grants will be made to the school boards, see ss. 96—99, *post*, and Chapter II., Part 1, Section 1 of the Revised Code of Regulations of the Education Department.

See s. 57, *post*, as to the power of the school board to borrow money on the security of the school fund and local rates.

Deficiency of school fund raised out of rates.

54. Any sum required to meet any deficiency in the school fund, whether for satisfying past or future liabilities, shall be paid by the rating authority out of the local rate.

The school board may serve their precept on the rating authority, requiring such authority to pay the amount specified therein to the treasurer of the school board out of the local rate, and such rating authority shall pay the same accordingly, and the receipt of such treasurer shall be a good discharge for the amount so paid, and the same shall be carried to the school fund.

If the rating authority have no moneys in their hands in respect of the local rate, they shall, or if they have paid the amount then for the purpose of reimbursing themselves they may, notwithstanding any limit under any Act of parliament or otherwise, levy the said rate, or any contributions thereto, or any increase of the said rate or contributions, and for that purpose shall have the same powers of levying a rate and requiring contributions as they have for the purpose of defraying expenses to which the local rate is ordinarily applicable.

As to the "local rate," see the third column of the first schedule to this Act.

The "rating authority" is the authority in regard to each district specified in the fourth column of the same schedule.

Section 35, *ante*, p. 31, enables the school board to appoint a treasurer.

The local authority may levy a separate rate in order to meet the precept of the school board; or they may raise the requisite amount by an addition to any rate they may make; that is to say, they may raise by means of the local rate a larger sum than they would require, but for the demand of the school board.

Apportionment of school fund in united and contributory district.

55. In a united district the school board shall apportion the amount required to meet the deficiency in the school fund among the districts constituting such united district in proportion to the rateable value of each such constituent district, and may raise the same by a precept sent to the rating authority of each constituent district.

Where one school district contributes to the expenses of the schools in another school district, the authority of the school owning district may send their precept either to the school board, if any, or to the rating authority of the contributing district, requiring them to pay to their treasurer the amount therein specified, and such authority or board shall pay the same accordingly, and the receipt of the treasurer shall be a good discharge for the same, and such amount, if paid by the school board, shall be paid out of the school fund.

The precept, if sent to the rating authority, either on the default of the school board or otherwise, shall be deemed to be a precept for meeting a deficiency in the school fund, and the provisions of this Act shall apply accordingly.

The provisions which are to apply accordingly, are those contained in s. 54, *ante*, p. 45.

Remedy of school board on default of rating authority, &c.

56. In either of the following cases, that is to say,

(1.) If the rating authority of any place make default in paying the amount specified in any precept of the school board; or

(2.) Where a school board require to raise a sum from any place which is part of a parish,

then, without prejudice to any other remedy, the school board may appoint an officer or officers to act within such place; and the officer or officers so from time to time appointed shall have within the said place, for the purpose of defraying the sum due from such place, all the powers of the rating authority of levying the local rate and any contributions thereto, and also all the powers of making and levying a rate which he or they would have if the said place were a parish, and such rate were a rate for the relief of the poor, and he or they were duly appointed an overseer or overseers of such parish, and he and they shall have such access to and use of the documents of the rating authority of such place relative to the local rate, and of all the valuation lists and rate books of the parish or parishes comprised in or comprising such place, as he or they may require.

Usually in the case of a divided parish, as between a county and a borough, the overseers are invested with authority to levy a separate rate on the part of the parish liable; under this section the school board are to appoint "an officer or officers" to act within such places, but no provision is made for payment of any salary to him, or for the audit of his account of his collection. It will obviously be impracticable for the officer to levy the exact sum required by the school boards, and the Act also fails to point out what he shall do with the excess, or to whom he shall account for it.

Reference must be made to the Poor Law Acts as to the powers of overseers of the poor to make and levy poor rates. Such Acts will be found in Glen's Poor Law Statutes, vols. 1 and 2.

Borrowing by school board.

57. Where a school board incur any expense in providing or enlarging a schoolhouse, they may, with the consent of the education department spread the payment over several years, not exceeding fifty, and may for that purpose borrow money on the security of the school fund and local rate, and may charge that fund and the local rate with the payment of the principal and interest due in respect of the loan. They may, if they so agree with the mortgagee, pay the amount borrowed, with the interest, by equal annual instalments, not exceeding fifty, and if they do not so agree, they shall annually

set aside one-fiftieth of the sum borrowed as a sinking fund.

10 & 11 Vict. c. 16.

For the purpose of such borrowing the clauses of "The Commissioners Clauses Act, 1847," with respect to the mortgages to be executed by the commissioners, shall be incorporated with this Act; and in the construction of those clauses for the purpose of this Act, this Act shall be deemed to be the special Act, and the school board which is borrowing shall be deemed to be the commissioners.

The public works loan commissioners may, on the recommendation of the education department, lend any money required under this section on the security of the school fund and local rate without requiring any further or other security, such loan to be repaid within a period not exceeding fifty years, and to bear interest at the rate of three and a half per centum per annum.

As to the provision of a sinking fund, see s. 84, of the Commissioners Clauses Act, 1847, in the Appendix, *post*.

The borrowing powers are contained in sections 75—88 of the same Act.

The provision for a sinking fund in section 57, *ante*, and section 84 of the Commissioners Clauses Act, 1847, will not apply when the loan is obtained from the public works loan commissioners.

Borrowing by school board for London.

58. Any sum borrowed by the school board for London in pursuance of this Act, with the approval of the education department, may be borrowed from and may be lent by the metropolitan board of works, and section thirty-seven of the Metropolitan Board of Works Loan Act, 1869, shall apply to such loan in the same manner as if the managers therein mentioned were the school board for London, and there were added to the sum therein authorised to be borrowed the sum authorised by the education department to be borrowed under this section.

The following is the section of the Act 32 & 33 Vict. c. 102 here referred to—

37. Where the managers of the metropolitan asylum dis-

trict, require to borrow money under "The Metropolitan Poor Act, 1867" and the Acts amending the same, such managers may borrow and the board may lend on the security authorized by those Acts such sums as the managers may have been authorized by the Poor Law Board, in pursuance of those Acts, to borrow, not exceeding in the whole five hundred thousand pounds.

For the purpose of raising the money so lent to the managers, the board may create consolidated stock under the provisions of this Act, in like manner and with the like sanction as they may create the same for the purpose of raising money for the purposes of the Acts mentioned in the first Schedule to this Act, and all the provisions of this Act shall apply as if such money were raised and stock were created for the purposes of the last-mentioned Acts, with this exception, that the money required in pursuance of this section, may be borrowed by the board in addition to the sum limited by this Act.

All sums received by the board from the said managers in respect of interest on or the principal of such loan shall be carried to the metropolitan consolidated loans fund.

Notwithstanding anything in the Metropolitan Poor Act, 1867, and the Acts amending the same, the amount so lent by the board shall be repaid to them by the said managers, with interest, within such period not exceeding sixty years as may be agreed upon between the board and the said managers, subject to the approval of the treasury.

The board may lend and the managers may borrow money in pursuance of this section for the purpose of repaying any loan due at the passing of this Act from the said managers.

The board and the said managers may execute all such deeds and documents and do all such acts as may be necessary or expedient for carrying this section into effect.

Accounts and Audit.

Accounts to be made up and examined.

59. The accounts of the school board shall be made up and balanced to the twenty-fifth of March and twenty-ninth of September in every year. The accounts shall be examined by the school board and signed by the chairman within fourteen days after the day to which they are made up.

As soon as practicable after the accounts are so signed they shall be audited.

How the examination of the accounts "by the school board" is to be made is not very apparent, at the best it will be perfunctory. No one but the chairman of the school board it seems can sign the account.

The district poor law auditors will doubtless be expected when they audit the accounts of the poor law authorities of the district to arrange for the audit of the accounts of the school board before they go to another part of their district on their audit circuit. It will, however, be a matter of no small difficulty to arrange the audits so that they may be held promptly after the balancing of the accounts; still, "as soon as practicable," it must be done.

Audit of accounts.

60. With respect to the audit of accounts of the school board the following provisions shall have effect:

(1.) The auditor shall be the auditor of accounts relating to the relief of the poor for the audit district in which the school district is situate, or if it is situate in more than one audit district by the auditor of such of the said audit districts as the poor law board may direct, and the term audit district in this provision shall be construed to include a parish for which an auditor is separately appointed to audit the accounts for the relief of the poor. The auditor shall receive such remuneration as the poor law board direct, and such remuneration, together with the expenses of or incident to the audit, shall be paid by the school board out of the school fund, and if unpaid may be recovered in a summary manner:

The Poor Law Board "direct," by an Order under seal, issued under the powers conferred upon them by the Poor Law Acts.

The construction in the section of the term audit district applies to the parishes of St. Marylebone, and St. Giles-in-the-Fields and St. George Bloomsbury, for which parishes auditors are separately appointed.

"The expenses of or incident to the audit," are such expenses as the auditor may be put to in travelling to the place of audit, if any such be incurred in addition to the expenses necessarily attendant upon his poor law audit circuit, which latter expenses are compensated for by his salary and allowances as poor law auditor.

See section 92, *post*, as to the recovery of money in a summary manner.

(2.) The audit shall be held at the office of the school board, or some other place sanctioned by the poor law board within the school district, or within the union within which the school district or some part thereof is situate, and at a time which is fixed by the auditor, but which shall be as soon as may be after the account is signed by the chairman:

"As soon as may be," must have reference to the district auditor's arrangements for poor law audits; and it will often necessarily be long after the accounts are signed by the chairman of the school board, that the auditor will be able to audit them.

(3.) The auditor at least fourteen days before holding the audit, shall serve on the school board, and publish notice of the time and place of holding the same:

The notice here mentioned will be published according to the directions, sections 80, 81 and 82, *post*; generally it will be difficult if not impracticable for the auditors to comply with subsection (2) of section 80, with regard to the publication of notices of audit on the church and chapel doors.

(4.) The clerk of the school board, or some person authorised by the school board, shall attend the audit, and produce to the auditor all books, bills, vouchers, and documents relating to the account:

(5.) Any ratepayer of the school district may be present at the audit, and may object to the account:

(6.) The auditor shall, as nearly as may be, have the like powers and be under the like obligation to allow and disallow items in the account, and to charge the school board, or any member or officer thereof, or any person accountable to them or him, with any sum for which they or he may be accountable, as in the case of an audit of the accounts relating to the relief of the poor in any union or parish; and any person aggrieved by the decision of the auditor shall have the like rights and remedies as in the case of such last-mentioned audit:

As to the powers of the auditor with regard to the audit of poor law accounts, see the statutes 7 & 8 Vict. c. 101, ss. 32, 33; 11 & 12 Vict. c. 91, ss. 5, 8, 9; 11 & 12 Vict. c. 103, ss. 9, 11, in the Appendix, *post*.

As regards the right of appeal against the auditor's decisions, see 7 & 8 Vict. c. 101, ss. 35, 36; and 11 & 12 Vict. c 91, s. 4, also in the Appendix.

The appeal in respect to allowances disallowances in surcharge in school board accounts, will be to the Court of Queen's Bench, or to the Poor Law Board.

(7.) The auditor shall have the like powers of requiring the attendance of persons, the production of books, bills, vouchers, and documents, and a declaration respecting vouchers and documents, as in the case of such last-mentioned audit; and any person who refuses or neglects to comply with any such requisition, or wilfully makes or signs a false declaration so required, shall be liable to the same penalties as in the case of such last mentioned audit:

As regards this sub-section see 7 & 8 Vict. c. 101, s. 33 in the Appendix, *post*.

(8.) Any moneys, books, documents, and chattels certified by the auditor to be due from any person may be recovered from such person in like manner as in the case of such last-mentioned audit, and the expenses incurred in such recovery shall be deemed to be part of the expenses of the audit:

See 7 & 8 Vict. c. 101, section 32 in the Appendix; and subsection (1) of this section, as to the expenses incident to the audit. As to the limitation of time for the recovery of certified sums, see 12 & 13 Vict. c. 103, s. 3, in the Appendix, *post*.

(9.) Subject to the provisions of this section, the poor law board may from time to time make such regulations as may be necessary respecting the form of keeping the accounts and the audit thereof.

Penalty for improper payment of surcharge.

61. Any member or officer of a school board, or manager appointed by them, who authorises or makes, or concurs in authorising or making, any payment or any entry in accounts for the purpose of defraying or making up to himself or any other person the whole or any part of any sum of money unlawfully expended from the school fund, or disallowed or surcharged by any auditor, shall, on summary conviction, be liable to pay a penalty not exceeding twenty pounds and double the amount of such sum.

Publication of accounts.

62. When the auditor has completed the audit he shall sign the balance sheet.

The school board shall cause a statement showing their receipts and expenditure to be printed in such form and with such particulars as may be from time to time prescribed by the education department, and shall send the same within thirty days after the balance sheet is signed by the auditor to each member of the rating authority, and to the overseers of every parish in the district, and to the education department; and the school board may, if they think fit, publish such statement or an abstract thereof in any local newspaper or newspapers circulating in the district, and shall furnish a copy of such statement to any ratepayer in the district, on his application, and on the payment of a sum not exceeding sixpence.

This section is directory as to sending a copy of the account to each member of the rating authority, and to the overseers, but it will not always be easy for the Board to ascertain the individual members of the rating authority specified in the fourth column of the first Schedule to the Act. The overseers are a rating authority composed of several members; but they are spoken of in the section as different from the rating authority; but they will only be so when the rating authority is another body.

Defaulting School Board.

Proceedings on default by school board.

63. Where the education department are, after such inquiry as they think sufficient, satisfied that a school board is in default as mentioned in this Act, they may by order declare such board to be in default, and by the same or any other order appoint any persons, not less than five or more than fifteen, to be members of such school board, and may from time to time remove any member so appointed, and fill up any vacancy in the number of such members, whether caused by removal, resignation, death or otherwise, and, subject as aforesaid, add to or diminish the number of such members.

After the date of the order of appointment the persons (if any) who were previously members of the school board shall be deemed to have vacated their offices as if they were dead, but any such member may be appointed a member by the education department. The members so appointed by the education department shall be deemed to be members of the school board in the same manner in all respects as if, by election or otherwise, they had duly become members of the school board under the other provisions of this Act, and may perform all the duties and exercise all the powers of the school board under this Act.

The members appointed by the education department shall hold office during the pleasure of the education department, and when that department consider that the said default has been remedied, and everything necessary for that purpose has been carried into effect, they may, by order, direct that members be elected for the school board in the same manner as in the case of the first formation of the school board. After the date fixed by any such order the members appointed by the education department shall cease to be members of the school board, and the members so elected shall be members of the school board in their room, but the members appointed by the education department shall not be disqualified from being so elected. Until any such order is made no person shall become a member of the school board otherwise than by the appointment of the education department.

Where a school board is not elected at the time fixed for the first election, or has ceased to be in existence, the education department may proceed in the same manner as if such board had been elected and were in existence.

As regards school boards in default, see sections 6, 10, 16, 18 and 32, *ante*.

The authority given to the education department when a school board is in default, is similar in its nature to the authority given by 29 & 30 Vict. c. 90, s. 49, to the secretary of state, when a local board of health, nuisance authority, or sewer authority, are in default in carrying into effect their respective powers.

On the contingency alluded to in the last paragraph of this section happening, the education department will proceed as in the case of a defaulting school board; as to such boards see ss. 6, 10, 16, 18 and 32, *ante*.

Certificate of education department as to appointment, expenses, and loans.

64. The education department may from time to time certify the appointment of any persons appointed to be members of a school board in default, and the amount of expenses that have been incurred by such persons, and the amount of any loan required to be raised for the purpose of defraying any expenses so incurred, or estimated as about to be incurred; and such certificate shall be conclusive evidence that all the requirements of this Act have been duly complied with, and that the persons so appointed have been duly appointed, and that the amounts therein mentioned have been incurred or are required.

Expenses incurred on default.

65. The expenses incurred in the performance of their duties by the persons appointed by the education department to be members of a school board, including such remuneration (if any) as the education department may assign to such persons, shall, together with all expenses incurred by the board, be paid out of the school fund; and any deficiency in the school fund may be raised by the school board as provided by this Act; and where the education department have, either before or after the payment of such expenses, certified that any expenses have been incurred by a school board, or any members appointed by them, such expenses shall be deemed to have been so incurred, and to have been properly paid out of the school fund.

Where the members of a school board have been appointed by the education department, such school board shall not borrow or charge the school fund with the principal and interest of any loan exceeding such amount as the education department certify as mentioned in this Act to be required.

The deficiency in the school fund will be raised, as provided by section 54, *ante*.

The certificate of the education department as to expenses

is the certificate referred to in the preceding part of this section.

66. Where the education department are of opinion that in the case of any school district the school board for such district are in default, or are not properly performing their duties under this Act, they may by order direct that the then members of the school board of such district shall vacate their seats, and that the vacancies shall be filled by a new election; and after the date fixed by any such order the then members of such board shall be deemed to have vacated their seats, and a new election shall be held in the same manner, and the education department shall take the same proceedings for the purpose of such election as if it were the first election; and all the provisions of this Act relating to such first election shall apply accordingly.

Dissolution of school boards.

The education department shall cause to be laid before both Houses of Parliament in every year a special report stating the cases in which they have made any order under this section during the preceding year, and their reasons for making such order.

As regards first elections under the Act, see sub-section (3), *ante*, p. 30.

Returns and Inquiry.

67. On or before the first day of January one thousand eight hundred and seventy-one, or in the case of the metropolis before the expiration of four months from the date of the election of the chairman of the school board, every local authority hereinafter mentioned, and subsequently any such local authority whenever required by the education department, but not oftener than once in every year, shall send to the education department a return containing

Returns by local authority.

such particulars with respect to the elementary schools and children requiring elementary education in their district as the education department may from time to time require.

Mode of obtaining returns.

68. For the purpose of obtaining such returns the education department shall draw up forms, and supply to the local authority such number of forms as may be required; and the managers or principal teacher of every school required to be included in any such return shall fill up the form, and return the same to the local authority within the time specified in that behalf in the form.

On the 16th, 18th, and 19th August, 1870, respectively the education department issued circulars addressed to the town clerk of each municipal borough, and to the overseers of each parish, calling for returns relating to school accommodation, in accordance with sections 67—72 of this Act. A copy of the Circular to the municipal boroughs, and of the forms of return will be found in the Appendix, *post*. The other Circulars are to the same effect, only altered to suit parishes.

Local authority to make returns.

69. The returns shall be made in the metropolis by the school board appointed under this Act, in boroughs by the council, and in every parish not situated in a borough or the metropolis by persons appointed for the purpose or by the overseers of such parish. Where a school board is formed under this Act, the returns shall be made by such school board within their district, instead of by the council, persons appointed as aforesaid, or overseers, as the case may be.

The persons appointed for the purpose may be appointed as follows; namely, the education department may, if they think fit, send to the overseers or other officers who have power to summon a vestry in such parish a requisition to summon, and such overseers or other officers shall summon, a vestry in such parish for the purpose of this section; and such vestry shall appoint two or more persons who shall be the local authority for the purpose of the returns under this Act.

The local authority may, with the sanction of the education department, employ persons to assist in making such returns, and may pay those persons such remuneration as the treasury may sanction. That remuneration, and all such other reasonable expenses incurred by the local authority in making such returns as the treasury may sanction, shall be paid by the education department.

Proceedings on default of authority to make returns.

70. If any local authority fail to make the returns required under this Act, the education department may appoint any person or persons to make such returns, and the person or persons so appointed shall for that purpose have the same powers and authorities as the local authority.

Inquiry by inspectors of education department.

71. The education department may appoint any persons to act as inspectors of returns, who shall proceed to inquire into the accuracy and completeness of any one or more returns made in pursuance of this Act, and into the efficiency and suitability of any school mentioned in any such return, or which ought to have been mentioned therein, and to inspect and examine the scholars in every such school. Where there is no return the inspector shall proceed as if there had been a defective return.

Refusal to fill up forms and to admit inspectors.

72. If the managers or teacher of any school refuse or neglect to fill up the form required for the said return, or refuse to allow the inspector to inspect the schoolhouse or examine any scholar, or examine the school books and registers, or make copies or extracts therefrom, such school shall not be taken into consideration among the schools giving efficient elementary education to the district.

Public Inquiry.

Public inquiry.

73. Where a public inquiry is held in pursuance of the provisions of this Act the following provisions shall have effect:

The provisions of the Act with respect to public inquiries are contained in section 9, *ante*, p. 8.

(1.) The education department shall appoint some person who shall proceed to hold the inquiry:

(2.) The person so appointed shall for that purpose hold a sitting or sittings in some convenient place in the neighbourhood of the school district to which the subject of inquiry relates, and thereat shall hear, receive, and examine any evidence and information offered, and hear and inquire into any objections or representations made respecting the subject of the inquiry, with power from time to time to adjourn any sitting.

Notice shall be published in such manner as the education department direct of every such sitting (except an adjourned sitting) seven days at least before the holding thereof:

Though the inquiry is to be in the "neighbourhood" of the school district, there seems nothing to prevent it from being held *within* the district.

(3.) The person so appointed shall make a report in writing to the education department setting forth the result of the inquiry, and stating his opinion on the subject thereof, and his reasons for such opinion, and the objections and representations, if any, made on the inquiry, and his opinion thereon; and the education department shall cause a copy of such report to be deposited with the school board (if any), or, if there is none, the town clerk of the borough or the churchwardens or overseers of the parishes to which the inquiry relates, and notice of such deposit to be published:

The notice of the deposit of the report upon the inquiry, pursuant to sub-section (3) will be published according to section 80, *post*. The education departments are to *cause* the notice to be published; but how they are so to cause it the section fails to say,—probably they will themselves publish it, and recover the cost as in sub-section (4).

(4.) The education department may make an order directing that the costs of the proceedings and inquiry shall be paid, according as they think just, either by the district as if they were expenses of a school board, or by the applicants for the inquiry; and such costs may be recovered, in the former case, as a debt due from the school board, or, if there is no school board, as a debt due from the rating authority, and, in the case of the applicants, as a debt due jointly and severally from them; and the education department may, if they think fit, before ordering the inquiry to be held, require the applicants to give security for such expenses, and in case of their refusal may refuse to order the inquiry to be held.

Attendance at School.

74. Every school board may from time to time, with the approval of the education department, **As to attendance of children at school.**

make byelaws for all or any of the following purposes:

As regards the enforcement of bye-laws under this section, see *post*, p. 64, and also section 92, *post*, as well as section 36, *ante*, p. 32.

(1.) Requiring the parents of children of such age, not less than five years nor more than thirteen years, as may be fixed by the byelaws, to cause such children (unless there is some reasonable excuse) to attend school:

As to what shall be a "reasonable excuse," see the second sub-sections (1), (2), and (3), *infra*.

(2.) Determining the time during which children are so to attend school; provided that no such byelaw shall prevent the withdrawal of any child from any religious observance or instruction in religious subjects, or shall require any child to attend school on any day exclusively set apart for religious observance by the religious body to which his parent belongs, or shall be contrary to anything contained in any Act for regulating the education of children employed in labour:

As regards the religious instruction of children in the school, see section 7, sub-sections (1) and (2), *ante*, p 6; and section 14, sub-section (2), *ante*, p. 11.

(3.) Providing for the remission or payment of the whole or any part of the fees of any child where the parent satisfies the school board that he is unable from poverty to pay the same:

See section 17, *ante*, as to school fees, and the remission of the same wholly or in part on the ground of poverty. When elementary schools are established, it will no longer be necessary for guardians of the poor to grant relief under 18 & 19 Vict. c. 34, s. 1, " for the purpose of enabling any poor person lawfully relieved out of the workhouse to provide education for any child of such person between the ages of four and sixteen, in any school to be approved of by the said guardians, for such time and under such conditions as the said guardians shall see fit."

As regards the boarding out of pauper children, see the 33 & 34 Vict c. 48, and the General Order issued by the Poor Law Board in pursuance of that statute.

(4.) Imposing penalties for the breach of any byelaws:

(5.) Revoking or altering any byelaw previously made.

Provided that any byelaw under this section requiring a child between ten and thirteen years of age to attend school shall provide for the total or partial exemption of such child from the obligation to attend school if one of Her Majesty's inspectors certifies that such child has reached a standard of education specified in such byelaw.

Any of the following reasons shall be a reasonable excuse; namely,

(1.) That the child is under efficient instruction in some other manner:

(2.) That the child has been prevented from attending school by sickness or any unavoidable cause:

(3.) That there is no public elementary school open which the child can attend within such distance, not exceeding three miles, measured according to the nearest road from the residence of such child, as the byelaws may prescribe.

The school board, not less than one month before submitting any byelaw under this section for the approval of the education department, shall deposit a printed copy of the proposed byelaws at their office for inspection by any ratepayer, and supply a printed copy thereof gratis to any ratepayer, and shall publish a notice of such deposit.

The notice will be published in accordance with the directions in section 80, *post*.

The education department before approving of any byelaws shall be satisfied that such deposit has been made and notice published, and shall cause such inquiry to be made in the school district as they think requisite.

Any proceeding to enforce any byelaw may be taken, and any penalty for the breach of any byelaw may be recovered in a summary manner; but no penalty imposed for the breach of any byelaw shall exceed such amount as with the costs will amount to five shillings for each offence, and such byelaws shall not come into operation until they have been sanctioned by Her Majesty in council.

See section 36, *ante*, p. 32, as to the appointment of an officer or officers to enforce byelaws under the Act, and also section 92, *post*.

It shall be lawful for Her Majesty, by order in Council, to sanction the said byelaws, and thereupon the same shall have effect as if they were enacted in this Act.

All byelaws sanctioned by Her Majesty in council under this section shall be set out in an appendix to the annual report of the education department.

The publication, in the Appendix to the Annual Report of the Education Department, of the byelaws of every elementary school will, in time, form an enormous mass of byelaws, considering that there are nearly fifteen thousand parishes in England having separate overseers appointed; for, certainly, upon an average, there will be at least one such school for each parish.

Miscellaneous.

75. Where any school or any endowment of a school was excepted from The Endowed Schools Act, 1869, on the ground that such school was at the commencement of that Act in receipt of an annual parliamentary grant, the governing body (as defined by that Act) of such school or endowment may frame and submit to the education department a scheme respecting such school or endowment. Application of small endowments.

The education department may approve such scheme with or without any modifications as they think fit.

The same powers may be exercised by means of such scheme as may be exercised by means of any scheme under the Endowed Schools Act, 1869; and such scheme, when approved by the education department, shall have effect as if it were a scheme made under that Act.

A certificate of the education department that a school was at the commencement of The Endowed Schools Act, 1869, in receipt of an annual parliamentary grant shall be conclusive evidence of that fact for all purposes.

By section 7 of the Endowed Schools Act, 1869 (32 & 33 Vict. c. 56), "the term 'governing body' means any body corporate, persons or person who have the right of holding, or any power of government of or management of any endowment, or, other than as master, over any endowed school, or have any power other than as master, of appointing officers, teachers, exhibitioners or others, either in an endowed school, or with emoluments out of any endowment."

By section 8 (3), the Act shall not apply "to any school which at the commencement of this Act (2nd August, 1869) is in receipt of an annual grant out of any sum of money appropriated by parliament to the civil service, intituled 'For Public Education in Great Britain,' or to the endowment thereof, unless such school is a grammar school, as defined by the Act of the session of the third and fourth years of the reign of Her present Majesty, chapter seventy-seven, or a school, a department of which only is in receipt of such grant."

By 3 & 4 Vict. c. 77, s. 25, "the word (*sic*) 'grammar school' shall mean and include all endowed schools, whether of royal or other foundation, endowed or maintained for the purpose of teaching Latin and Greek, or either of such languages, whether in the instrument of foundation or endowment, or in the statutes or decree of any court of record, or in any Act of parliament establishing such school, or in any other evidences or documents such instruction shall be expressly described, or shall be described by the word 'grammar,' or any other form of expression which is or may be construed as intending Greek or Latin, and whether by such evidences or documents as aforesaid, or in practice such instruction be limited exclusively to Greek or Latin, or extended to both such languages, or to any other branch or branches of literature or science in addition to them or either of them;" and "the words 'grammar school' shall not include schools not endowed, but shall mean and include all endowed schools which may be grammar schools by reputation, and all other charitable institutions and trusts so far as the same may be for the purpose of providing such instruction as aforesaid."

The powers of the commissioners as to the reorganization of endowed schools are contained in sections 9 to 30, inclusive of the Endowed Schools Act, 1869.

Inspection of voluntary schools by inspector not one of Her Majesty's inspectors.

76. Where the managers of any public elementary school not provided by a school board desire to have their school inspected or the scholars therein examined, as well in respect of religious as of other subjects, by an inspector other than one of Her Majesty's inspectors, such managers may fix a day or days not exceeding two in any one year for such inspection or examination.

The managers shall, not less than fourteen days before any day so fixed cause public notice of the day to be given in the school, and notice in writing of such day to be conspicuously affixed in the school.

On any such day any religious observance may be practised, and any instruction in religious subjects given at any time during the meeting of the school, but any scholar who has been withdrawn by his parent from any religious observance or instruction in religious subjects shall not be required to attend the school on any such day.

77. Where a parish is situated partly within and partly without a borough, the part situate outside of the borough shall be taken to be for all the purposes of this Act, except as otherwise expressly mentioned, a parish by itself, and the ratepayers thereof may meet in vestry in the same manner in all respects as if they were the inhabitants of a parish; every such meeting, and also the meeting for the purposes of this Act of the ratepayers of any parish (the ratepayers of which have not usually met in vestry), shall be deemed to be a vestry, and, save as provided by this Act, be subject to the Act of the fifty-eighth year of the reign of King George the Third, chapter sixty-nine, and the Acts amending the same, and, subject as aforesaid, shall be summoned by the persons and in the mode prescribed by the education department; and the overseers of the whole parish shall be deemed to be the overseers of any such part of a parish.

Parish divided by boundaries of boroughs.

The Vestries Act, 58 Geo. 3, c. 69, is amended by the 59 Geo. 3, c. 85; 1 Vict. c. 45; and 16 & 17 Vict. c. 65. The whole of these Acts will be found in Glen's Parish Vestries Acts, fourth edition.

78. The education department shall, for the purposes of The Charitable Trusts Acts, 1853 to 1869, be deemed to be persons interested in any elementary school to which those Acts are applicable, and the endowment thereof.

Education department may apply to charity commissioners under 16 & 17 Vict. c. 137, &c.

With regard to this section, see section 22, *ante*, p. 20, and the note thereon.

Ascertaining rateable value.

79. The rateable value of any parish or school district shall for the purposes of this Act be the rateable value as stated in the valuation lists, if any, and if there are none, then as stated in the rate book for the time being in force in such parish and in the parishes constituting the district; and the overseers and other persons having the custody of such valuation lists and rate book shall, when required by the school board, produce such lists and rate book to the school board, and allow the school board and any person appointed by them to inspect the same, and take copies of or extracts therefrom.

As to the custody of valuation lists, see 31 & 32 Vict. c. 122, s. 30; and 32 & 33 Vict. c. 67, s. 68, in Glen's Poor Law Statutes.

The valuation lists mentioned in this section are the valuation lists approved by the assessment committee, and in force for the time being. It is the poor *rate* that is in force and not the rate book, which may contain many rates. The last poor rate duly made, allowed, and published, is the rate which is in force, and it remains in force till another is made. The latter part of this section was introduced in the House of Lords.

Mode of publication of notices.

80. Notices and other matters required by this Act to be published shall, unless otherwise expressly provided, be published,—

(1.) By advertisement in some one or more of the newspapers circulating in the district or place to which such notice relates:

(2.) By causing a copy of such notices or other matter to be published to be affixed, during not less than twelve hours in the day, on Sunday on or near the principal doors of every church and chapel in such district or place to which notices are usually affixed, and at every other place in such district or place at which notices are usually affixed.

The mode only and not the time of publication is here mentioned. It will, however, suffice if the publication, whether in a newspaper or on the church doors on Sunday, be, when no time is mentioned, some reasonable time before the event is to take place to which the notice has reference.

81. Certificates, notices, requisitions, orders, precepts, and all documents required by this Act to be served or sent may, unless otherwise expressly provided, be served and sent by post, and, till the contrary is proved, shall be deemed to have been served and received respectively at the time when the letter containing the same would be delivered in the ordinary course of post; and in proving such service or sending it shall be sufficient to prove that the letter containing the certificate, notice, requisition, order, precept, or document was prepaid, and properly addressed, and put into the post.

Notices may be served by post.

82. Certificates, notices, requisitions, orders, and other documents may be served on a school board by serving the same on their clerk, or by sending the same to or delivering the same at the office of such board.

Notices to and by school board.

No express power is given to the school board by the Act to provide an office, but the expense of providing an office would be an expense payable out of the school fund, under section 53, *ante*, p. 44.

Certificates, notices, requisitions, orders, precepts, and other documents may be in writing or in print, or partly in writing and partly in print, and if requiring authentication by a school board may be signed by their clerk.

See 31 & 32 Vict. c. 37, s. 2, in the Appendix, *post*, as to proof of handwriting of signature not being required.

83. All orders, minutes, certificates, notices, requisitions, and documents of the education department, if purporting to be signed by some secretary or assistant secretary of the education department, shall, until the contrary is proved, be deemed to have been so signed and to have been made by the education department, and may be proved by the

Evidence of orders, &c., of education department.

production of a copy thereof purporting to have been so signed.

The Documentary Evidence Act, 1868, shall apply to the education department in like manner as if the education department were mentioned in the first column of the schedule to that Act, and any member of the education department, or any secretary or assistant secretary of the education department, were mentioned in the second column of that schedule.

See the Documentary Evidence Act, 31 & 32 Vict. c. 37, in the Appendix, *post*. This sub-section was added in the House of Lords.

Effect of requisitions of education department.

84. After the expiration of three months from the date of any order or requisition of the education department under this Act such order or requisition shall be presumed to have been duly made, and to be within the powers of this Act, and no objection to the legality thereof shall be entertained in any legal proceeding whatever.

Appearance of school board.

85. A school board may appear in all legal proceedings by their clerk, or by some member of the board authorised by a resolution of the board; and every such resolution shall appear upon the minutes of the proceedings of the board, but every such resolution shall, until the contrary is proved, be deemed in any legal proceeding to appear upon such minutes.

Tenure of teacher and his removal from house under sects. 17 & 18 of 4 & 5 Vict. c. 38.

86. The provisions of the School Sites Acts with respect to the tenure of the office of the schoolmaster or schoolmistress, and to the recovery of possession of any premises held over by a master or mistress who has been dismissed or ceased to hold office, shall extend to the case of any school provided by a school board, and of any master or mistress of such school, in the same manner as if the school

board were the trustees or managers of the school as mentioned in those Acts.

The School Sites Acts will be found in the Appendix, *post*.

87. Every ratepayer in a school district may at all reasonable times, without payment, inspect and take copies of and extracts from all books and documents belonging to or under the control of the school board of such district.

Ratepayer may inspect books, &c., of school board.

Any person who hinders a ratepayer from so inspecting or taking copies of or extracts from any book or document, or demands a fee for allowing him so to do, shall be liable, on summary conviction, to a penalty not exceeding five pounds for each offence.

See the definition of the term "ratepayer," *ante*, p. 4, and note thereon.

88. If any returning officer, clerk, or other person engaged in an election of a school board under this Act wilfully makes or causes to be made an incorrect return of the votes given at such election, every such offender shall, upon summary conviction, be liable to a penalty not exceeding fifty pounds.

Penalty for making incorrect return.

As regards the appointment of officers to conduct elections of school boards, see Article 1 of the first part of the second schedule, *post*.

89. If any person wilfully personates any person entitled to vote in the election of a school board under this Act, or answers falsely any question put to him in voting in pursuance of an order made under the second schedule to this Act, or falsely assumes to act in the name or on the behalf of any person so entitled to vote, he shall be liable, on summary conviction, for every such offence to a penalty not exceeding twenty pounds.

Penalty on personation of voter.

Penalty for forging or falsifying any voting paper or obstructing the election.

90. If any person knowingly personate and falsely assume to vote in the name of any person entitled to vote in any election under this Act, or forge or in any way falsify any name or writing in any paper purporting to contain the vote or votes of any person voting in any such election, or by any contrivance attempt to obstruct or prevent the purposes of any such election, or wilfully contravene any regulation made by the education department under the second schedule to this Act with respect to the election, the contravention of which is expressed to involve a penalty, the person so offending shall upon summary conviction be liable to a penalty of not more than fifty pounds, and in default of payment thereof to be imprisoned for a term not exceeding six months.

Corrupt practices.

91. Any person who at the election of any member of a school board or any officer appointed for the purpose of such election is guilty of corrupt practices shall, on conviction, for each offence be liable to a penalty not exceeding two pounds, and be disqualified for the term of six years after such election from exercising any franchise at any election under this Act, or at any municipal or parliamentary election.

The term corrupt practices in this section includes all bribery, treating, and undue influence which under any Act relating to a parliamentary election renders such election void.

The provisions in sections 89 and 90 of this Act, it will be seen, are much more stringent than those in 14 & 15 Vict. c. 105, s. 3, with regard to malpractices at elections of guardians.

The following Acts by the Corrupt Practices Prevention Act, 1854, (17 & 18 Vict. c. 102), are "bribery, treating, and undue influence."

Bribery by the Briber.

I.—1. Every person who shall

2. Directly—indirectly—by himself—by any person on his behalf

3. Give—lend—agree to give—agree to lend—offer—promise—promise to procure—promise to endeavour to procure
4. Any money—any valuable consideration
5. To or for any voter—to or for any person on behalf of any voter—to or for any other person
6. In order to induce any voter to vote or refrain from voting—corruptly on account of any voter having voted or refrained from voting.

II.—1. Every person who shall
2. Directly—indirectly—by himself—by any other person on his behalf
3. Give—procure—agree to give—agree to procure—offer—promise—promise to procure—promise to endeavour to procure
4. Any office—any place—any employment
5. To or for any voter—to or for any person on behalf of any voter—to or for any other person.
6. In order to induce such voter to vote or refrain from voting—corruptly on account of any voter having voted or refrained from voting.

III.—1. Every person who shall make
2. Directly—indirectly—by himself—by any other person on his behalf
3. Any such gift—loan—offer—promise—procurement—or agreement as aforesaid
4. To or for any person
5 In order to induce such person
6. To procure—to endeavour to procure
7. The return of any person—the vote of any voter.

IV.—1. Every person who shall
2. Advance—pay—cause to be paid
3. Any money
4. To any other person—to the use of any other person
5. With the intent that
6. Such money—any part of such money
7. Shall be expended in bribery.

V.—1. Every person who shall
2. Knowingly pay—knowingly cause to be paid
3. Any money
4. To any person
5. In discharge—in repayment
6. Of money wholly or in part extended in bribery.

Bribery by the Bribed.

I.—1. Every person who shall upon or in consequence of
2. Any gift — loan—offer — promise—procurement—agreement
3. Procure—engage—promise to procure—endeavour to procure
4. The return of any person—the vote of any voter.

II.—1. Every voter who shall
2. Before any election—during any election
3. Directly—indirectly—by himself—by any other person on his behalf
4. Receive—agree for—contract for
5. Any money—gift—loan—valuable consideration—office—place—employment
6. For himself—for any other person
7. For voting—for agreeing to vote—for refraining from voting—for agreeing to refrain from voting.

III.—1. Every person who shall after any election
2. Directly—indirectly—by himself—by any other person on his behalf
3. Receive
4. Any money—any valuable consideration
5. On account of
6. Any person having voted—any person having refrained from voting—having induced any other person to vote or to refrain from voting.

Treating.

1. Every candidate at an election who shall *corruptly*
2. By himself—by any person—with any person—by any ways or means on his behalf
3. At any time before any election—at any time during any election—at any time after any election
4. Directly—indirectly
5. Give—provide—cause to be given—cause to be provided—be accessary to the giving or providing—pay wholly or in part any expenses incurred for
6. Any meat—any drink—any entertainment — any provision.
7. To or for any person
8. In order to be elected—for being elected—for the purpose of corruptly influencing such person to give or refrain from giving his vote—for the purpose of corruptly influencing any other person to give or refrain from giving his vote—on account of such person having voted or refrained from voting—on account of such person being about to vote or refrain from voting.

Recovery of penalties.

92. Any penalty and any money which under this Act is recoverable summarily, and all proceedings under this Act which may be taken in a summary manner, may be recovered and taken before two justices in manner directed by an Act of the session of the eleventh and twelfth years of the reign of Her present Majesty, chapter forty-three, intituled "An Act to facilitate the performance of the duties of justices of the peace out of sessions within England and Wales with respect to summary convictions and orders," and the Acts amending the same.

11 & 12 Vict. c. 43.

This section was introduced in the House of Lords. The Act 11 & 12 Vict. c. 43, will be found at length with notes of the cases decided upon it in the fourth edition of Glen's Jervis's Acts.

Provision as to Oxford.

93. In the case of the borough of Oxford, the provisions of this Act relating to boroughs shall be construed as if the local board were therein mentioned instead of the council; if a school board is formed in the borough of Oxford, one-third of the school board shall be elected by the university of Oxford, or the colleges and halls therein, in such manner as may be directed by the education department by an order made under the power contained in the second schedule to this Act.

The local board of Oxford is the local board under the Local Government Act, 1858, (21 & 22 Vict. c. 98) which by section 82 of that Act, consists of Vice Chancellor of the University of Oxford, and the Mayor of Oxford for the time being, and forty-five other commissioners, fifteen to be elected by the University of Oxford, sixteen by the town council of Oxford, and fourteen by the rate payers of the parishes situated within the jurisdiction of the Oxford commissioners. See Glen's Law of Public Health and Local Government, p. 27, fifth edition.

By this section the local board of Oxford are substituted for the council of the borough, in respect of any application to the education department under section 12 (1), *ante*, p. 10. See also section 31, *ante*, p. 29, as to the election of school boards.

Effect of schedules.

94. The schedules to this Act shall be of the same force as if they were enacted in this Act, and the Acts mentioned in the fourth schedule to this Act may be cited in the manner in that schedule mentioned.

Returns by school board.

95. Every school board shall make such report and returns and give such information to the education department as the department may from time to time require.

(II.) Parliamentary Grant.

Parliamentary grant to public elementary school only.

96. After the thirty-first day of March one thousand eight hundred and seventy-one no parliamentary grant shall be made to any elementary school which is not a public elementary school within the meaning of this Act.

See the definition of a public elementary school, section 7, *ante*, p. 6.

No parliamentary grant shall be made in aid of building, enlarging, improving, or fitting up any elementary school, except in pursuance of a memorial duly signed, and containing the information required by the education department for enabling them to decide on the application, and sent to the education department on or before the thirty-first day of December one thousand eight hundred and seventy.

As the school boards under this Act are enabled to build, enlarge, and fit up elementary schools at the charge of the rate payers of the respective districts, hence this provision, that all parliamentary grants for such purposes shall cease, unless the preliminary steps to obtain such grants are taken on or before the 31st December, 1870.

The conditions on which building grants for elementary schools are made by the education department are contained in Chapter I. of the Revised Code of Regulations; but are too voluminous to be here inserted.

Conditions of annual parliamentary grant.

97. The conditions required to be fulfilled by an elementary school in order to obtain an annual par-

liamentary grant shall be those contained in the minutes of the education department in force for the time being, and shall amongst other matters provide that after the thirty-first day of March one thousand eight hundred and seventy-one—

(1.) Such grant shall not be made in respect of any instruction in religious subjects:

(2.) Such grant shall not for any year exceed the income of the school for that year which was derived from voluntary contributions, and from school fees, and from any sources other than the parliamentary grant;

but such conditions shall not require that the school shall be in connexion with a religious denomination, or that religious instruction shall be given in the school, and shall not give any preference or advantage to any school on the ground that it is or is not provided by a school board:

Provided that where the school board satisfy the education department that in any year ending the twenty-ninth of September the sum required for the purpose of the annual expenses of the school board of any school district, and actually paid to the treasurer of such board by the rating authority, amounted to a sum which would have been raised by a rate of threepence in the pound on the rateable value of such district, and any such rate would have produced less than twenty pounds, or less than seven shillings and sixpence per child of the number of children in average attendance at the public elementary schools provided by such school board, such school board shall be entitled, in addition to the annual parliamentary grant in aid of the public elementary schools provided by them, to such further sum out of moneys provided by parliament as, when added to the sum actually so paid by the rating authority, would, as the case may be, make up the sum of twenty pounds, or the sum of seven shillings and sixpence for each such child, but no attendance shall be reckoned for the purpose of calculating such average attendance unless it is an attendance as defined in the said minutes:

Provided that no such minute of the education department not in force at the time of the passing of this Act shall be deemed to be in force until it has lain for not less than one month on the table of both Houses of parliament.

The proviso to this section was inserted in the House of Lords. The regulations as to grants to maintain schools are contained in the Second Chapter of the Code, which can be procured (price 3*d.*) from the publishers of this work.

Refusal of grant to unnecessary schools.

98. If the managers of any school which is situate in the district of a school board acting under this Act, and is not previously in receipt of an annual parliamentary grant, whether such managers are a school board or not, apply to the education department for a parliamentary grant, the education department may, if they think that such school is unnecessary, refuse such application.

The education department shall cause to be laid before both houses of parliament in every year a special report stating the cases in which they have refused a grant under this section during the preceding year, and their reasons for each such refusal.

Power of schools to take parliamentary grants.

99. The managers of every elementary school shall have power to fulfil the conditions required in pursuance of this Act to be fulfilled in order to obtain a parliamentary grant, notwithstanding any provision contained in any instrument regulating the trusts or management of their school, and to apply such grant accordingly.

Report.

Annual report of education department.

100. The education department shall in every year cause to be laid before both houses of parliament a report of their proceedings under this Act during the preceding year.

FIRST SCHEDULE (*a*).

School District.	School Board.	Local Rate.	Rating Authority.
The metropolis -	The school board appointed under this Act.	In the City of London the consolidated rate (*b*).	The commissioners of sewers.
		In the parishes mentioned in schedule A. and the districts mentioned in schedule B. to the Metropolis Management Act, 1855, the general rate, and fund raised by the general rate (*c*).	In the parishes the vestry, and in the districts the district board.
		In places mentioned in schedule C. to the said Act, the rate levied for the purposes of the Metropolitan Poor Act, 1867, and any Act amending the same (*d*).	The masters of the bench, treasurer, governors, or other persons who have the chief control or authority in such place.
Boroughs, except Oxford.	The school board appointed under this Act.	The borough fund or borough rate (*e*).	The council.
District of the local board of Oxford.	The school board appointed under this Act.	Rate leviable by the local board (*f*).	The local board.
Parishes not included in any of the above-mentioned districts.	The school board appointed under this Act.	The poor rate (*g*)	The overseers (*h*).

(*a*) See section 4, *ante*, p. 5, and section 37 (10), *ante*, p. 36, and section 94, *ante*, p. 76.
(*b*) See 32 & 33 Vict. c. 102, s. 22
(*c*) See 18 & 19 Vict. c. 120, s. 158.
(*d*) See 30 Vict. c. 6, s. 66.
(*e*) See 5 & 6 Will. 4, c. 76, ss, 48, 92.
(*f*) See 28 & 29 Vict. c. 108, s. 8.
(*g*) See 43 Eliz. c. 2, s. 1.
(*h*) The term "overseer" will include the churchwardens in the case of a parish. See 43 Eliz. c. 2, s. 1, in Glen's Poor Law Statutes.

SECOND SCHEDULE (*a*).

First Part.

Rules respecting Election and Retirement of Members of a School Board.

1. The election of a school board shall be held at such time, and in such manner, and in accordance with such regulations as the education department may from time to time by order prescribe, and the education department may by order appoint or direct the appointment of any officers requisite for the purpose of such election, and do all other necessary things preliminary or incidental to such election: Provided, that any poll shall be taken in the metropolis in like manner as a poll is taken under "The Metropolis Management Act, 1855," and shall be taken in any other district in like manner as a poll of burgesses or ratepayers (as the case may be) is usually taken in such district.

The Act nowhere prescribes the qualification required for a member of a school board, neither does it enable the education department to prescribe any qualification. It seems that the candidate need not be a ratepayer within the district, nor, indeed, need he reside within a district. The Act does not say in what manner persons shall be nominated; but doubtless the regulations which may be issued by the education department will provide the mode of nominating candidates.

However they may be nominated, the candidates will not be nominated for particular parishes, but for the whole district, and they will be elected by the electors of the whole district; and the votes will be given in accordance with section 29, *ante*, p. 27.

As regards the taking a poll in the metropolis, see sections 21—27 of 18 & 19 Vict. c. 120, in the Appendix, *post*.

By 5 & 6 Will. 4, c. 76, s. 29, every burgess who shall be enrolled on the burgess roll for the time being of the borough shall be entitled to vote in the election of councillors, and no person who shall not be enrolled in such burgess roll shall have

(*a*) See section 31 (2), *ante*, p. 29.

any voice or be entitled to vote in such election. With regard to the mode of taking the poll of burgesses, see sections 32—37 of that Act.

A poll of the vestry is taken under the 58 Geo. 3, c. 69, as to which see Glen's Parish Vestries Acts, fourth edition.

With regard to offences and malpractices at the election, see sections 88—91, *ante*.

As to elections in Oxford, see section 93, *ante*, p. 75.

As to females voting at the election of a school board, see note to section 37, sub-section 6, *ante*, p. 35.

2. The expenses of the election and taking the poll in any district other than the metropolis shall be paid by the school board out of the school fund.

As regards the school fund, see section 53, *ante*, p. 44.

3. An order made by the education department under the power contained in this part of this schedule shall, as regards any election held before the first day of September one thousand eight hundred and seventy-one, be deemed to be within the powers of this schedule, and to have been duly made and have effect as if it were enacted in this schedule, but shall not be of any force as regards any election after the said date unless it has been confirmed by parliament.

The order of the education department as regards any elections held after the 1st September, 1871, to be of any validity must be confirmed by an Act of parliament.

4. Any such order so far as relates to the metropolis shall supersede any provisions contained in the Acts relating to the election of common councilmen, and in the Metropolis Management Act, 1855, and the Acts amending the same.

5. If from any cause no members are elected at the time at which they ought to be elected in accordance with this Act, then—

(*a.*) In the case of the first election the education department may appoint another day for the election, or may proceed as in the case of a school board in default;

(*b*.) In the case of a triennial election the retiring members, or so many as are willing to serve, shall be deemed to be re-elected, or, if all the retiring members refuse to serve, the education department may appoint another day for the election, or may proceed as in the case of a school board in default.

As to school boards in default, see section 32, *ante*, p. 30, and section 63, *ante*.

6. If an insufficient number of members are elected, or if, in the case of no members being elected, some of the retiring members are and some are not willing to serve, the school board, so far as it is constituted, shall elect a person to fill each vacancy.

7. No election under this Act shall be questioned on the ground of the title of the returning officer, or any person presiding at the poll, or any officer connected with the election.

8. Notice of the election of a person to be a member of the school board shall be sent to that person by the returning officer: in the case of the first election such notice shall be accompanied by a summons to attend the first meeting of the school board at the prescribed time.

9. The day for the triennial retirement of members shall be the prescribed day.

See Article 19, *post*, as to the term "prescribed."

10. The first members shall retire from office on the day for retirement which comes next after the expiration of three years from the day fixed for the first election.

11. Members chosen to fill the offices of retiring members shall come into office on the day for retirement, and shall hold office for three years only.

This means members chosen to fill the offices vacated by retiring members.

12. Any person who ceases to be a member of the

school board shall, unless disqualified as hereinafter mentioned, be re-eligible.

13. A member of the school board may resign on giving to the board one month's previous notice in writing of his intention so to do.

14. If a member of the school board absents himself during six successive months from all meetings of the board, except from temporary illness or other cause to be approved by the board, or is punished with imprisonment for any crime, or is adjudged bankrupt, or enters into a composition or arrangement with his creditors, such person shall cease to be a member of the school board, and his office shall thereupon be vacant.

It seems that a member who absents himself from the meetings of the school board from *permanent* illness will not necessarily vacate his office.

The word "crime" will include a felony or misdemeanor; but imprisonment for not obeying an order of justices will not be imprisonment for a "crime."

15. If any casual vacancy in office occurs by death, resignation, disqualification, or otherwise, an election shall be held in manner directed by an order made under the power contained in this part of this schedule.

As to such order, see Articles 1 and 3 of this Schedule, *ante*.

16. If by any means the number of members of a school board is reduced to less than the number required for a quorum, the education department may proceed as if such board were a board in default, or may direct an election to be held to fill up the vacancies in manner directed by an order made under the power contained in this part of this schedule.

As to a quorum of members, see the third schedule, Article 1 (*d*), *post*, p. 87, as to school boards in default, see sections 32 and 63, *ante;* and as to the order of the education department, see Articles 1 and 3 of this Schedule, *ante*.

17. The member chosen to fill up a casual vacancy

shall retain his office so long only as the vacating member would have retained the same if no vacancy had occurred.

18. If the number of the board is reduced in pursuance of the provisions of this Act, the chairman of the board shall at some meeting, as soon as may be after such reduction, determine by ballot on the members who shall retire, so as to reduce the number of the board to the number to which it is so reduced.

See section 39, *ante*, p. 37, as to the reduction of the number of members forming a school board.

19. The term "prescribed" in this schedule means prescribed by some minute or order of the education department.

Second Part.

Rules respecting Resolutions for Application for School Board.

1. The meeting of a council for the purpose of passing such a resolution shall be summoned in the manner in which a meeting of the council is ordinarily summoned, and the resolution shall be passed by a majority of the members present and voting on the question.

As regards applications by town councils for school boards see section 12, *ante*, p. 10.

The mayor of a borough has power to call an extraordinary meeting at any time he may think proper, by causing a notice signed by himself to be fixed on the Town Hall three days before the day of the intended meeting, stating the time and place thereof. (See *Rex* v. *Thomas*, 8 A. & E. 183.) And in case the mayor shall refuse to call any meeting after a requisition for the purpose, signed by five members of the council at the least, shall have been presented to him, it shall be lawful for the said five members to call a meeting of the council by giving a notice, to be signed by them instead of the mayor, and stating therein the business proposed to be transacted at such meeting; and in every case a summons to attend the council, specifying the business proposed to be transacted at such meeting, signed by the town clerk, shall be left at the usual place of abode of every member of the council, or at the premises in respect of which he is enrolled as a burgess three clear days at least before such meeting; and no business shall be transacted at such meeting other than is specified in the notice. (5 & 6 Will. 3, c. 76, s. 69.) If the members present and voting on the question be equally divided, the chairman of the meeting shall have a casting vote. *Ibid.*

2. The resolution passed by the persons who would elect the school board shall be passed in like manner as near as may be as that in which a member of the school board is elected, with such necessary modifications as may be contained in any order made under the powers of the first part of this schedule, and such powers shall extend to the passing of the resolution in like manner as if it were an election, but the expenses incurred with reference to such a resolution shall be paid by the overseers out of the poor rate.

As regards the applications for school boards referred to in this Article, see section 12, *ante*, p. 10; and as to the mode of passing the resolution, see the first part of this Schedule, Article 1, and the note thereon.

3. If a resolution is rejected, the resolution shall not be again proposed until the lapse of twelve months from the date of such rejection.

See, however section 10, *ante*, p. 9, as to the powers of the educational department with regard to the formation of school boards by that department.

Third Part.

Rules for Election of School Board in Metropolis.

1. If any person be returned for more than one division he shall, at or before the first meeting of the school board after such election, signify in writing to the board his decision as to the division which he

may desire to represent on such return, and if he fails so to do the school board shall decide the division which he shall represent; and upon any such decision the office of member for the other division shall be deemed vacant. Such vacancy shall be filled up by an election to be held in manner directed by an order made under the power contained in the first part of this schedule.

2. The provisions in the first part of this schedule shall apply in the case of the school board in the metropolis.

3. The provisions in the first part of this schedule with respect to the proceedings in the case of no members being elected for a school district shall not only apply to the whole of the metropolis, but shall apply to the case of no members being elected for any particular division, with this qualification, that the education department shall not proceed as in the case of a school board in default, but may direct that persons may be elected by the school board to be members for such division.

4. In the places named in schedule (C.) to "The Metropolis Management Act, 1855," the expenses of the election shall be paid out of the local rate, and such rate, or any increase of the rate, may be levied for the purpose.

5. The day for the retirement of members from office shall be the first day of December.

6. Any casual election shall be held on the day fixed by the school board, and shall be an election for the division a member for which has created the vacancy.

7. If any vacancy is filled up by the school board the election shall be by the whole school board.

THIRD SCHEDULE (*a*).

Proceedings of School Board.

1. The board shall meet for the despatch of business, and shall from time to time make such regulations with respect to the summoning, notice, place, management, and adjournment of such meetings, and generally with respect to the transaction and management of business, including the quorum at meetings of the board, as they think fit, subject to the following conditions:—

(*a.*) The first meeting shall be held on the third Thursday after the election of the board, and if not held on that day shall be held on some day to be fixed by the education department:

(*b.*) Not less than one ordinary meeting shall be held in each month; one meeting shall be held as soon as possible after every triennial election of members:

(*c.*) An extraordinary meeting may be held at any time on the written requisition of three members of the board addressed to the clerk of the board:

(*d.*) The quorum to be fixed by the board shall consist of not less than three members, and in the case of the metropolis not less than nine members:

(*e.*) Every question shall be decided by a majority of votes of the members present and voting on that question:

(*f.*) The names of the members present as well

(*a*) See section 30 (6), *ante*, p. 29; and section 94, p. 76.

as of those voting upon each question, shall be recorded:

(*g*.) No business involving the appointment or dismissal of a teacher, any new expense, or any payment (except the ordinary periodical payments), or any business which under this Act requires the consent of the education department, shall be transacted unless notice in writing of such business has been sent to every member of the board seven days at least before the meeting.

2. The board shall at their first meeting, and afterwards from time to time at their first meeting after each triennial election, appoint some person to be chairman, and one other person to be vice-chairman, for the three years for which the board hold office.

3. If any casual vacancy occurs in the office of chairman or vice-chairman the board shall, as soon as they conveniently can after the occurrence of such vacancy, choose one of their members to fill such vacancy, and every such chairman or vice-chairman so elected as last aforesaid shall continue in office so long only as the person in whose place he may be so elected would have been entitled to continue if such vacancy had not happened.

4. If at any meeting the chairman is not present at the time appointed for holding the same the vice-chairman shall be the chairman of the meeting, and if neither the chairman nor vice-chairman shall be present then the members present shall choose some one of their number to be chairman of such meeting.

5. In case of an equality of votes at any meeting the chairman for the time being of such meeting shall have a second or casting vote.

6. All orders of the board for payment of money, and all precepts issued by the board, shall be

deemed to be duly executed if signed by two or more members of the board authorized to sign them by a resolution of the board, and countersigned by the clerk; but in any legal proceeding it shall be presumed, until the contrary is proved, that the members signing any such order or precept were authorized to sign them.

7. The appointment of any officer of the board may be made by a minute of the board, signed by the chairman of the board, and countersigned by the clerk (if any) of the board, and any appointment so made shall be as valid as if it were made under the seal of the board.

8. Precepts of the board may be in the form given at the end of this schedule.

Proceedings of Managers appointed by a School Board.

The managers may elect a chairman of their meetings. If no such chairman is elected, or if the chairman elected is not present at the time appointed for holding the same, the members present shall choose one of their number to be chairman of such meeting. The managers may meet and adjourn as they think proper. The quorum of the managers shall consist of such number of members as may be prescribed by the school board that appointed them, or, if no number be prescribed, of three members. Every question at a meeting shall be determined by a majority of votes of the members present and voting on that question, and in case of an equal division of votes the chairman shall have a second or casting vote.

The proceedings of the managers shall not be invalidated by any vacancy or vacancies in their number.

See section 15, *ante* p. 12, as to the latter part of this Schedule.

Form of Precept.

School district of   to wit.

To the council [*or* overseers, *&c.*] of the borough [*or* parish] of   .   These are to require you, the council [*or* overseers] of the borough [*or* parish] of   , from and out of the moneys in the hands of your treasurer [*or* your hands], to pay on or before the   day of   into the hands of *A. B.*, treasurer of the school board of the said district, the sum of   being the amount required for the expenses of the said school board up to the   of   18   ; and if there are no moneys in the hands of your treasurer [*or* your hands] to raise the same by means of a rate.

(Signed) *C. D.*, } Members of the school board
E. F., } of the district of   .
G. H., clerk of the said school board.

FOURTH SCHEDULE (a).

SCHOOL SITES ACTS.

The following Acts may be cited together as the "School Sites Acts, 1841 to 1851."

Year and Chapter of Act.	Title of Act.	Short Title by which Acts may be cited.
4 & 5 Vict. c. 38	An Act to afford further facilities for the conveyance and endowment of sites for schools.	The School Sites Act, 1841.
7 & 8 Vict. c. 37	An Act to secure the terms on which grants are made by Her Majesty out of the parliamentary grant for the education of the poor; and to explain the Act of the fifth year of Her present Majesty, for the conveyance of sites for schools.	The School Sites Act, 1844.
12 & 13 Vict. c. 49	An Act to extend and explain the provisions of the Acts for the granting of sites for schools.	The School Sites Act, 1849.
14 & 15 Vict. c. 24	An Act to amend the Acts for the granting of sites for schools.	The School Sites Act, 1851.

FIFTH SCHEDULE (b).

DIVISIONS OF METROPOLIS.

Name of Division.	Name of Division.
Marylebone.	Westminster.
Finsbury.	Southwark.
Lambeth.	City.
Tower Hamlets.	Chelsea.
Hackney.	Greenwich.

(a) See section 20, *ante*, p. 19, and section 94, p. 76 with regard to this Schedule.

(b) See section 37 (1), *ante*, p. 33; section 39, p. 37; and section 94, p. 74, with regard to the divisions of the metropolis.

APPENDIX.

I.—SCHOOL SITES ACTS (*a*).

4 & 5 VICT. CAP. 38.

An Act to afford further facilities for the Conveyance and Endowment of Sites for Schools.

[21st June, 1841.]

WHEREAS it is expedient that greater facilities should be given for the erection of schools and buildings for the purposes of education: May it therefore please your Majesty that it may be enacted; and be it enacted by the Queen's most excellent Majesty, by and with the advice and consent of the Lords spiritual and temporal, and Commons, in this present parliament assembled, and by the authority of the same, that from and after the passing of this Act an Act passed in the session held in the sixth and seventh years of the reign of His late Majesty King William the Fourth, intituled "An Act to facilitate the Conveyance of Sites for Schoolrooms," shall be and the same is hereby repealed; provided that all matters and things done in pursuance of the said Act shall be and remain valid as though the said Act was not repealed; and all matters and things commenced in pursuance of the said Act shall be continued according to the provisions of this Act, if the same shall be applicable, otherwise shall be continued conformably to the said recited Act, which shall be deemed to be still in force with regard to such proceedings.

Repeal of 6 & 7 Will. 4, 3. 70; but things done in pursuance thereof declared valid, and those commenced to be continued according to this Act.

(*a*) See section 20, *ante*, p. 19.

Landlords empowered to convey land to be used as sites for schools, &c.

2. And be it enacted, that any person being seised in fee simple, fee tail, or for life, of and in any manor or lands of freehold, copyhold, or customary tenure, and having the beneficial interest therein, or in Scotland being the proprietor in fee simple or under entail, and in possession for the time being, may grant, convey, or enfranchise by way of gift, sale, or exchange, in fee simple or for a term of years, any quantity not exceeding one acre of such land, as a site for a school for the education of poor persons, or for the residence of the schoolmaster or schoolmistress, or otherwise for the purposes of the education of such poor persons in religious and useful knowledge; provided that no such grant made by any person seised only for life of and in any such manor or lands shall be valid, unless the person next entitled to the same in remainder in fee simple or fee tail (if legally competent) shall be a party to and join in such grant: Provided also, that where any portion of waste or commonable land shall be gratuitously conveyed by any lord or lady of a manor for any such purposes as aforesaid the rights and interests of all persons in the said land shall be barred and divested by such conveyance: Provided also, that upon the said land so granted as aforesaid, or any part thereof, ceasing to be used for the purposes in this Act mentioned, the same shall thereupon immediately revert to and become a portion of the said estate held in fee simple or otherwise, or of any manor or land as aforesaid, as fully to all intents and purposes as if this Act had not been passed, anything herein contained to the contrary notwithstanding.

Chancellor and council of the Duchy of Lancaster empowered to grant lands to the trustees of any existing or intended school.

3. And whereas it may be expedient and proper that the chancellor and council of Her Majesty's Duchy of Lancaster, on Her Majesty's behalf, should be authorized to grant, convey, or enfranchise, to or in favour of the trustee or trustees of any existing or intended school, lands and hereditaments belonging to Her Majesty in right of Her said duchy, for the purposes of this Act: Be it therefore enacted, that it shall and may be lawful for the chancellor and council of Her Majesty's Duchy of Lancaster for the time being, by any deed or writing under the hand and seal of the chancellor of the said duchy for the time being, attested by the clerk of the council of the said duchy for the time being, for and in the name of Her Majesty, Her heirs and successors, to

grant, convey, or enfranchise, to or in favour of such trustee or trustees, any lands and hereditaments to be used by them for the purposes of this Act, upon such terms and conditions as to the said chancellor and council shall seem meet; and where any sum or sums of money shall be paid as or for the purchase or consideration for such lands or hereditaments so to be granted, conveyed, or enfranchised as aforesaid, the same shall be paid by such trustee or trustees into the hands of the receiver-general for the time being of the said duchy, or his deputy, and shall be by him paid, applied, and disposed of according to the provisions and regulations contained in an Act passed in the Forty-eighth year of the reign of His late Majesty King George the Third, intituled "An Act to improve the land Revenue of the Crown in England, and also of His Majesty's Duchy of Lancaster," or any other Act or Acts now in force for that purpose: Provided always, that upon the said land so granted as aforesaid, or any part thereof, ceasing to be used for the purposes in this Act mentioned, the same shall thereupon immediately revert to and become again a portion of the possessions of the said duchy, as fully to all intents and purposes as if this Act or any such grant as aforesaid had not been passed or made, anything herein contained to the contrary notwithstanding.

48 Geo. 3, c. 73.

If lands cease to be used for the purposes of the Act they shall revert.

4. And be it enacted, that for the purposes of this Act only, and for such time only as the same shall be used for the purposes of this Act, it shall be lawful for any two of the principal officers of the Duchy of Cornwall, under the authority of a warrant issued for that purpose under the hands of any three or more of the special commissioners for the time being for managing the affairs of the duchy of Cornwall, or under the hands of any three or more of the persons who may hereafter for the time being have the immediate management of the said duchy, if the said duchy shall be then vested in the Crown, or if the said duchy shall then be vested in a Duke of Cornwall then under the hand of the chancellor for the time being of the said duchy, or under the hands of any three or more of the persons for the time being having the immediate management of the said duchy, by deed under their hands, to grant and convey to the trustees or trustee for the time being of any existing school, or of any school intended to be established by

Officers of the Duchy of Cornwall empowered, upon sufficient authority, to grant lands to the trustees of any existing or intended school.

virtue of this Act, any lands, tenements, or hereditaments forming part of the possessions of the said Duchy of Cornwall, not exceeding in the whole one acre in any one parish, upon such terms and conditions as to the said special commissioners or chancellor, or such other persons as aforesaid, shall seem meet: Provided always, that upon the said land so granted as aforesaid, or any part thereof, ceasing to be used for the purposes in this Act mentioned, the same shall thereupon immediately revert to and become again a portion of the possessions of the said duchy, as fully to all intents and purposes as if this Act or any such grant as aforesaid hath not been passed or made, anything herein contained to the contrary notwithstanding.

If lands cease to be used for the purposes of the Act they shall revert.

Persons under disability empowered to convey lands for the purposes of this Act.

5. And be it enacted, that where any person shall be equitably entitled to any manor or land, but the legal estate therein shall be in some trustee or trustees it shall be sufficient for such person to convey the same for the purposes of this Act without the trustee or trustees being party to the conveyance thereof; and where any married woman shall be seised or possessed of or entitled to any estate or interest, manorial or otherwise, in land proposed to be conveyed for the purposes of this Act, she and her husband may convey the same for such purposes by deed, without any acknowledgment thereof; and where it is deemed expedient to purchase any land for the purposes aforesaid belonging to or vested in any infant or lunatic, such land may be conveyed by the guardian or committee of such infant, or the committee of such lunatic respectively, who may receive the purchase money for the same, and give valid and sufficient discharges to the party paying such purchase money, who shall not be required to see to the application thereof.

Corporations, justices, trustees, &c. empowered to convey lands for the purposes of this Act.

6. And be it enacted, that it shall be lawful for any corporation, ecclesiastical or lay, whether sole or aggregate, and for any officers, justices of the peace, trustees or commissioners holding land for public, ecclesiastical, parochial, charitable, or other purposes or objects, subject to the provisions next hereinafter mentioned, to grant, convey, or enfranchise, for the purposes of this Act, such quantity of land as aforesaid in any manner vested in such corporation, officers, justices, trustees, or commissioners: provided always, that no ecclesiastical

corporation sole, being below the dignity of a bishop, shall be authorized to make such grant without the consent in writing of the bishop of the diocese to whose jurisdiction the said ecclesiastical corporation is subject: provided also, that no parochial property shall be granted for such purposes without the consent of a majority of the ratepayers and owners of property in the parish to which the same belongs, assembled at a meeting to be convened according to the mode pointed out in the Act passed in the sixth year of the reign of His late Majesty, intituled "An Act to facilitate the Conveyance of Workhouses, and other Property of Parishes and of Incorporations or Unions of Parishes in England and Wales," and without the consent of the poor law commissioners, to be testified by their seal being affixed to the deed of conveyance, and of the guardians of the poor of the union within which the said parish may be comprised, or of the guardians of the poor of the said parish where the administration of the relief of the poor therein shall be subject to a board of guardians, testified by such guardians being the parties to convey the same; provided also, that where any officers, trustees, or commissioners, other than parochial trustees, shall make any such grant, it shall be sufficient if a majority or quorum authorized to act of such officers, trustees, or commissioners, assembled at a meeting duly convened, shall assent to such grant, and shall execute the deed of conveyance, although they shall not constitute a majority of the actual body of such officers, trustees, or commissioners: provided also, that the justices of the peace may give their consent to the making any grant of land or premises belonging to any county, riding, or division by vote at their general quarter sessions, and may direct the same to be made in the manner directed to be pursued on the sale of the sites of gaols by an Act passed in the seventh year of the reign of His late Majesty George the Fourth, intituled "An Act to authorize the Disposal of unnecessary Prisons in England."

5 & 6 Will. 4, c. 69.

7 Geo. 4, c. 18.

Grants of land may be made to corporations or trustees, to be held by them for school purposes.

7. And be it enacted, that all grants of land or buildings, or any interest therein, for the purposes of the education of poor persons, whether taking effect under the authority of this Act or any other authority of law, may be made to any corporation sole or aggregate, or to several corporations sole, or to any trustees whatsoever, to be held by such corporation or corporations or trus-

tees for the purposes aforesaid: provided nevertheless, that any such grant may be made to the minister of any parish being a corporation, and the churchwardens or chapelwardens and overseers of the poor, or to the minister and kirk session of the said parish and their successors; and in such case the land or buildings so granted shall be vested for ever thereafter in the minister, churchwardens, or chapelwardens, and overseers of the poor, for the time being, or the minister and kirk session of such parish, but the management, direction, and inspection of the school shall be and remain according to the provisions contained in the deed of conveyance thereof; provided also, that where any ecclesiastical corporation sole below the dignity of a bishop shall grant any land to trustees, other than the minister, churchwardens or chapelwardens, and overseers, for the purposes aforesaid, such trustees shall be nominated in writing by the bishop of the diocese to whose jurisdiction such corporation shall be subject; provided that where any school shall be intended for any ecclesiastical district, not being a parish as hereinafter defined, it shall be sufficient if the grant be made to the minister and church or chapelwarden or wardens of the church or chapel of such district, to hold to them and their successors in office; and such grant shall enure to vest the land, subject to the conditions contained in the deed of conveyance, in such minister and the church or chapel warden or wardens for the time being.

Estates now vested in trustees for the purposes of education may be conveyed to the minister and churchwardens.

8. And whereas schools for the education of the poor in the principles of the established church, or in religious and useful knowledge, and residences for the masters or mistresses of such schools, have been heretofore erected, and are vested in trustees not having a corporate character: be it therefore enacted, that it shall be lawful for the trustees for the time being of such last-mentioned schools and residences, not being subject to the provisions of the Act passed in the last session of parliament, intituled "An Act for improving the Conditions and extending the Benefits of Grammar Schools," to convey or assign the same, and all their estate and interest therein, to such ministers and churchwardens and overseers of the poor of the parish within which the same are respectively situate, and their successors as aforesaid, or, being situate within an ecclesiastical district not being a parish as hereinafter defined, then to

the minister and church or chapelwardens of the church or chapel of such district, and their successors, in whom the same shall thereafter remain vested accordingly, but subject to and under the existing trusts and provisions respectively affecting the same.

Any number of sites may be granted for separate schools.

9. And be it enacted, that any person or persons or corporation may grant any number of sites for distinct and separate schools, and residence for the master or mistress thereof, although the aggregate quantity of land thereby granted by such person or persons or corporation shall exceed the extent of one acre; provided that the site of each school and residence do not exceed that extent; provided also, that not more than one such site shall be in the same parish.

Form of grants, &c.

10. And be it enacted, that all grants, conveyances, and assurances of any site for a school, or the residence of a schoolmaster or schoolmistress, under the provisions of this Act, in respect of any land, messsuages, or buildings, may be made according to the form following, or as near thereto as the circumstances of the case will admit; (that is to say,)

"I, [*or* we, *or the corporate title of a corporation*], under the authority of an Act passed in the year of the reign of Her Majesty Queen Victoria, intituled 'An Act for affording further Facilities for the Conveyance and Endowment of Sites for Schools,' do hereby freely and voluntarily, and without any valuable consideration [*or* do, in consideration of the sum of , to me *or* us *or* the said paid,] grant, [alienate,] and convey to , all [*description of the premises*], and all [my *or* our *or* the right, title, and interest of the] to and in the same and every part thereof, to hold unto and to the use of the said , and his *or* their [heirs *or* executors *or* administrators *or* successors], for the purposes of the said Act, and to be applied as a site for a school for poor persons of and in the parish of , and for the residence of the schoolmaster [*or* schoolmistress [of the said school, [*or for other purposes of the said school*], and for no other purpose whatever; such school to be under the management and control of [*set forth the mode in which and the persons by whom the school is to be managed, directed, and inspected*]. *In case the school be conveyed to trustees, a clause providing for the renewal of the trustees, and in cases where the land is purchased, exchanged, or demised, usual covenants or obligations for title, may be added.*] In witness whereof the conveying and other parties have hereunto set their hands and seals, this day of .

"Signed, sealed, and delivered by the said , in the presence of , of ."

And no bargain and sale or livery of seisin shall be requisite in any conveyance intended to take effect under the provisions of this Act, nor more than one witness to the execution by each party; and instead of such attestation such conveyance of any lands or heritages in Scotland shall be executed with a testing clause, according to the law and practice of Scotland; and, being recorded within sixty days of the date thereof in the general register of seisins or particular register for the county or stewartry in which the lands or heritages lie, shall, without actual seisin, be valid and effectual in law to all intents and purposes, and shall be a complete bar to all other rights, titles, trusts, interests, and incumbrances to, in, or upon the lands or heritages so conveyed.

Application of purchase money for land sold by any ecclesiastical corporation sole.

11. And be it enacted, that where any land shall be sold by any ecclesiastical corporation sole for the purposes of this Act, and the purchase money to be paid shall not exceed the sum of twenty pounds, the same may be retained by the party conveying, for his own benefit; but when it shall exceed the sum of twenty pounds it shall be applied for the benefit of the said corporation, in such manner as the bishop in whose diocese such land shall be situated shall, by writing under his hand, to be registered in the registry of his diocese, direct and appoint; but no person purchasing such land for the purpose aforesaid shall be required to see to the due application of any such purchase money.

Application of purchase money for land sold in Scotland.

12. And be it enacted, that the price of any lands or heritages to be sold for the purposes of this Act by any heir of entail or other incapacitated person or persons in Scotland shall be applied and invested in such and the like manner as is directed in relation to any money awarded to be paid for lands or heritages belonging to heirs of entail or incapacitated persons under an Act passed in the first and second years of the reign of His

late Majesty King William the Fourth, intituled "An Act for amending and making more effectual the Laws concerning Turnpike Roads in Scotland."

1 & 2 Will. 4, c. 43.

Ecclesiastical corporations to procure a certificate as to the extent of the land conveyed.

13. And be it enacted, That when any ecclesiastical corporation sole below the dignity of a bishop shall grant any land belonging to him in right of his corporation for the purposes of this Act, he shall procure a certificate, under the hands of three beneficed clergymen of the diocese within which the land to be conveyed shall be situate, as to the extent of the land so conveyed, to be endorsed on the said deed; which certificate shall be in the form following; (that is to say,)

Form of certificate.

"We, *A. B.* clerk, rector of the parish of *C. D.* clerk, rector of the parish of and *E. F.* clerk, vicar of the parish of being three beneficed clergymen of the diocese of do hereby certify, that clerk, rector of the parish of within the said diocese of being about to convey a portion of land situate in the said parish of for the purposes of a school, under the powers of the Act passed in the year of the reign of Her Majesty Queen Victoria, intituled 'An Act for affording further facilities for the conveyance and endowment of sites for schools,' we have at his request inspected and examined the portion of land, and have ascertained that the same is situate at [*here describe the situation*], and that the extent thereof does not exceed acre . As witness our hands, this day of at in the county of and diocese of . Witness of ."

And until such certificate shall have been signed no such conveyance shall have any force or validity.

Trustees empowered to sell or exchange lands or buildings.

14. And be it enacted, That when any land or building shall have been or shall be given or acquired under the provisions of the said first-recited Act or this Act, or shall be held in trust for the purposes aforesaid, and it shall be deemed advisable to sell or exchange the same for any other more convenient or eligible site, it shall be lawful for the trustees in whom the legal estate in the said land or building shall be vested, by the direction or with the consent of the managers and directors of the said school, if any such there be, to sell or exchange

the said land or building, or part thereof, for other land or building suitable to the purposes of their trust, and to receive on any exchange any sum of money by way of effecting an equality of exchange, and to apply the money arising from such sale or given on such exchange in the purchase of another site, or in the improvement of other premises used or to be used for the purposes of such trust; provided that where the land shall have been given by any ecclesiastical corporation sole the consent of the bishop of the diocese shall be required to be given to such sale or exchange before the same shall take place: Provided also, that where a portion of any parliamentary grant shall have been or shall be applied towards the erection of any school, no sale or exchange thereof shall take place without the consent of the secretary of state for the home department for the time being.

All conveyances of land under 6 & 7 W. 4, c. 70, to be deemed effectual for vesting the fee simple.

15. And whereas in many cases conveyances of land have been made, purporting to be made in pursuance of the powers of the said first-recited Act, to the minister or incumbent and the churchwardens or chapelwardens of certain parishes or places, as and for sites of schools or houses of residence for the schoolmasters; and doubts have been entertained whether such conveyances are valid and effectual for the purposes of conveying the fee simple, in consequence of the said statute not containing any words of limitation to the successors of such persons: Be it therefore enacted, That all conveyances whereby any land shall have been conveyed to the minister or incumbent and the churchwardens or chapelwardens of any parish or place for the time being, whether made to them as such minister or incumbent and churchwardens or chapelwardens, or to them and their successors, shall be deemed and taken to have been and shall be valid and effectual for the purpose of vesting the fee simple, or such other estate as hath been proposed to be conveyed, in the persons who from time to time shall be the minister or incumbent and the churchwardens or chapelwardens of such place, such minister being the rector, vicar, or perpetual curate, whether endowed or not, of the said parish or place.

Certain conveyances of

16. And whereas certain lands or buildings have been conveyed for valuable consideration, upon trust for

the purposes of the education of the poor, and through inadvertence or other causes the deeds or assurances conveying the same have not been enrolled in Chancery as required by the Act passed in the ninth year of the reign of His late Majesty King George the Second, intituled "An Act to restrain the disposition of lands whereby the same become unalienable," and by the said herein-before first-recited Act: Be it therefore enacted, That notwithstanding the said provisions all such conveyances shall be and remain valid for the space of twelve calendar months next ensuing the passing of this Act, and if enrolled in Chancery before the expiration of that time shall be and remain valid hereafter as if duly enrolled within the time required by the provisions of the said Acts: Provided nevertheless, that no effect shall be given hereby to any deed or other assurance heretofore made, so far as the same has been already avoided by any suit at law or in equity, or by any other legal or equitable means whatsoever, or to affect or prejudice any suit at law or in equity actually commenced for avoiding any such deed or other assurance, or for defeating the charitable uses in trust or for the benefit of which such deed or other assurance may have been made.

lands, &c., for purposes of education not enrolled as required by the 9 G. 2, c. 36, rendered valid if enrolled within 12 months from the passing of this Act.

Proviso for deeds avoided in any suit.

17. And be it enacted, That no schoolmaster or schoolmistress to be appointed to any school erected upon land conveyed under the powers of this Act shall be deemed to have acquired an interest for life by virtue of such appointment, but shall, in default of any specific engagement, hold his office at the discretion of the trustees of the said school.

No schoolmaster to acquire a life interest by virtue of his appointment.

18. And for the more speedy and effectual recovery of the possession of any premises belonging to any school which the master or mistress who shall have been dismissed, or any person who shall have ceased to be master or mistress, shall hold over after his or her dismissal or ceasing to be master or mistress, be it enacted, That when any master or mistress, not being the master or mistress of any grammar school within the provision of the Act of the last session of parliament hereinafter mentioned, holding any schoolroom, schoolhouse, or any other house, land, or tenement, by virtue of his or her office, shall have been dismissed or removed, or shall have ceased to be master or mistress, and shall neglect

Justices of the peace or sheriffs to give possession of schoolrooms, &c., in case of the refusal of the master.

or refuse to quit and deliver up possession of the premises within the space of three calendar months after such dismissal or ceasing to be master or mistress, not having any lawful authority for retaining such possession, it shall be lawful for the justices of the peace acting for the district or division in which such premises are situated, in petty sessions assembled, or any two of them, or for the sheriff of the county in Scotland, and they are hereby required, on the complaint of the trustees or managers of the said school, or some one of them, on proof of such master or mistress having been dismissed or removed, or having ceased to be such master or mistress, to issue a warrant under their hands and seals, or under the hand of such sheriff in Scotland, to some one or more of the constables and peace officers of the said district or division or of the sheriff's officers in Scotland, commanding him or them, within a period to be therein named, not less than ten nor more than twenty-one clear days from the date of such warrant, to enter into the premises, and give possession of the same to the said trustees or managers or their agents, such entry and possession being given in England in such manner as justices of the peace are empowered to give possession of any premises to any landlord or his agent under an Act passed in the second year of the reign of Her present Majesty, intituled "An Act to facilitate the Recovery of Possession of Tenements after due Determination of the Tenancy."

1 & 2 Vict. c. 74.

Powers granted to the commissioners under 3 & 4 Vict. c. 60, for applying land to Ecclesiastical purposes extended to land granted by way of gift.

19. And whereas by an Act passed in the last session of parliament, intituled "An Act to further amend the Church Building Acts," provision was made to enable Her Majesty's commissioners for building new churches to apply land in any parish granted to them for any of the purposes of the Church Building Acts to any other ecclesiastical purposes, or for the purpose of any parochial or charitable school, or any other charitable or public purpose relating to any such parish or place: And whereas through an accidental omission such provision does not extend to cases of land granted by way of gift: Be it therefore enacted, That such power so given to the said commissioners, so far as it is applicable to the purposes of any school, shall extend to every case of land granted, given, or conveyed to them under the authority of the several Acts in the said Act recited.

20. And be it enacted, That the term "parish" in this Act shall be taken to signify every place separately maintaining its own poor, and having its own overseers of the poor and church or chapel wardens. Definition of the term "parish."

21. And be it enacted, That this Act shall not extend to Ireland. Act not to extend to Ireland.

22. And be it enacted, That nothing herein contained shall repeal or affect an Act passed in the second year of the reign of Her present Majesty, intituled "An Act to facilitate the Foundation and Endowment of additional Schools in Scotland," or another Act passed in the last session of parliament, intituled "An Act to enable Proprietors of entailed Estates in Scotland to feu or lease on long Leases Portions of the same for the building of Churches and Schools, and for Dwelling-Houses and Gardens for the Ministers and Masters thereof." Act not to affect 1 & 2 Vict. c. 87, or 3 & 4 Vict. c. 48.

23. And be it enacted, That this Act may be altered or amended by any Act to be passed in this session of Parliament. Act may be amended, &c. this session.

---

7 & 8 VICT. CAP. 37.

An Act to secure the Terms on which Grants are made by Her Majesty out of the Parliamentary Grant for the Education of the Poor; and to explain the Act of the Fifth Year of the Reign of Her present Majesty, for the Conveyance of Sites for Schools.

[19th July, 1844.]

WHEREAS during several years last past divers sums of money have been granted by parliament to Her Majesty, to be applied for the purpose of promoting the education of the poor in Great Britain, and similar grants may hereafter be made: And whereas Her Majesty hath appointed a committee of Her council to receive applications for assistance from such grants, and to report thereon, and to advise Her as to the terms and conditions upon which such assistance shall be granted, and many such reports have been made and approved of by Her

Majesty, and the terms and conditions having been assented to by the applicants, grants have been made out of the said fund: And whereas in some cases, by reason of the deeds of endowment of schools in respect of which such applications have been received having been executed before the grant has been made, such terms and conditions have not and cannot be made permanently binding on the estate; but the parties promoting the said schools have entered into personal obligations or assurances for the due performance of such terms and conditions, though deriving no beneficial interest from the charitable institution which they have established; and it is desirable to provide permanent security to Her Majesty and her successors for the due fulfilment of the terms and conditions, and to relieve the parties from the personal liabilities so entered into for the purpose aforesaid: Be it therefore enacted by the Queen's most excellent Majesty, by and with the advice and consent of the Lords spiritual and temporal, and Commons, in this present parliament assembled, and by the authority of the same, that where any grant hath been made or shall hereafter be made out of any sums of money heretofore granted or hereafter to be granted by parliament for the purposes of education in Great Britain, under the advice of any committee of the council on education for the time being, upon terms and conditions to provide for the inspection of the school by an inspector appointed or to be appointed by Her Majesty and her successors, which shall not be inserted in the conveyance of the site of the school, or in the deed declaring the trusts thereof, and such grant shall be made in aid of the purchase of the site, or of the erection, enlargement, or repair of the school, or of the residence of the master or mistress thereof, or of the furnishing of the school, such terms and conditions shall be binding and obligatory upon the trustees or managers of the said school or other the premises for the time being, in like manner and to the like effect as though they had been inserted in the conveyance of the site of the said school, or in the declaration of the trusts thereof; and henceforth all personal obligations entered into for the purpose of securing the fulfilment of such terms and conditions shall, so far as they relate thereto, but no further, be null and void: Provided nevertheless, that such terms and conditions shall have been or shall be set set forth in some docu-

The terms and conditions upon which parliamentary aid has been given towards the building of schools secured upon the site.

ment in writing, signed by the trustees of the said school or the major part of them, or by the party or parties conveying the site, in the case where there shall have been a voluntary gift thereof.

2. And whereas there are many endowments for the purpose of education of the poor in Great Britain of ancient date, the schools whereon have become dilapidated, and, the funds of such endowment being insufficient for the restoration thereof, application is made by the trustees, or by the persons acting in the discharge of the trusts thereof, for aid out of the said parliamentary grant, but the same hath been declined, because such applicants could not impose upon their lawful successors in the said trust the conditions which the said committee would have advised Her Majesty to require to secure the due inspection of such schools, and it is expedient to enable them to do so: Be it therefore enacted, that where the major part or the trustees of any endowed school for the education of the poor duly appointed under the terms of the deed of endowment, or, when such deed cannot be found or cannot be acted upon, of the persons who shall be in the possession of the endowment, and shall be acting in the execution of the trusts or the reputed trusts thereof, shall, and in cases where there shall be a visitor of such school with the consent of such visitor in writing, apply for aid out of such parliamentary grant to enable them to rebuild, repair, or enlarge the school belonging to such endowment, or the residence of the master or mistress thereof, or to furnish such school, and shall in writing assent to the said school being open to inspection on behalf of Her Majesty and Her successors, if the said committee shall deem fit to advise that any such grant shall be made, it shall immediately after the making of such grant, and thenceforth from time to time, be lawful for any inspector of schools appointed by Her Majesty and her successors, in conformity with the terms contained in the writing testifying such consent as aforesaid, to enter the said school at all reasonable hours in the day for the purpose of inspecting and examining the state and condition of the school and scholars thereat, and of making such report thereon, as he shall deem fit.

The terms upon which aid shall be granted to trustees of ancient endowed schools.

3. And whereas by an Act passed in the fifth year of

Death of donor within

twelve calendar months not to avoid grant.
9 G. 2, c. 36.

the reign of Her present Majesty, intituled "An Act to afford further Facilities for the Conveyance and Endowment of Sites for Schools," it is enacted that any person, being seised in fee simple, fee tail, or for life of and in any manor, or lands of freehold, copyhold, or customary tenure, may grant, convey, or enfranchise, and subject to the provisions therein mentioned, any quantity not exceeding one acre of land as a site for a school or otherwise, as therein likewise specified; and it is desirable to prevent any such grant, being of so limited an interest, from being defeated by the death of the grantor: Be it enacted, that where any deed shall have been or shall be executed under the powers and for the purposes contained in the said Act, without any valuable consideration, the same shall be and continue valid, if otherwise lawful, although the donor or grantor shall die within twelve calendar months from the execution thereof.

Site may be granted to the minister and churchwardens.

4. And whereas it was provided by the said Act that grants of land or buildings, or any interest therein, for the purposes of the education of poor persons, might be made to the minister of any parish, being a corporation, and the churchwardens or chapelwardens and overseers of the poor and their successors, and it is sometimes found inexpedient or impracticable to introduce the overseers as parties to the legal estate: Be it therefore enacted, that such grants may be made to the minister and churchwardens of any parish, such minister being the rector, vicar, or perpetual curate thereof, whether endowed or not, to hold to them and their successors, subject to the provisions contained in the deed of conveyance thereof for the management, direction, and inspection of the school and premises.

Rector, vicar, or perpetual curate may grant to the minister and churchwardens, or to the minister, churchwardens, and overseers of his parish.

5. And be it enacted, that if the rector, vicar, or perpetual curate of any parish shall be desirous of making a grant of any land for the purposes and under the powers of the said Act, being part of the glebe or other possessions of his benefice, and shall, with the consent of the patron of the said benefice, and of the bishop of the diocese within which the same shall be situated, grant the same to the minister and church or chapel wardens, or to the minister, church or chapel wardens, and overseers of the poor of the said parish, such grant shall be valid, and shall thenceforth enure for the purposes of the trust set forth therein, if otherwise lawful

notwithstanding such minister is the party making the grant.

6. And be it enacted, that this Act may be altered by any other Act in this session of parliament. Act may be altered this session.

---

12 & 13 VICT. CAP. 49.

An Act to extend and explain the Provisions of the Acts for the granting of Sites for Schools.

[28th July, 1849.]

WHEREAS by an Act passed in the fifth year of the reign of Her Majesty provisions are made for facilitating the erection of schools and buildings for the education of poor persons, which said Act hath been since explained and extended by an Act of the eighth year of the reign of Her Majesty; and it is expedient that further facilities should be afforded for the conveyance of lands for sites for schools in cases where such lands are comprised with other lands in leases, and that some amendments should also be made in the said Acts: be it therefore enacted by the Queen's most excellent Majesty, by and with the advice and consent of the Lords spiritual and temporal, and Commons, in this present parliament assembled, and by the authority of the same, that if part only of any lands comprised in a lease for a term of years unexpired shall be conveyed or agreed to be conveyed for the purposes of the said firstly herein-before mentioned Act, the rent payable in respect of the lands comprised in such lease, and any fine certain or fixed sum of money to be paid upon any renewals thereof, or either of such payments, may be apportioned between the part of the said lands so conveyed or agreed to be conveyed and the residue thereof; and such apportionment may be settled by agreement between the parties following, that is to say, the lessor or other the owner subject to such lease of the lands comprised therein, the lessee or other the party entitled thereto by virtue of such lease or any assignment thereof for the residue of the term therereby created, and the party to whom such conveyance as aforesaid for the purposes of the said firstly hereinbefore

Where part only of lands under lease conveyed, the rent and fine upon renewal of lease may be apportioned.

mentioned Act is made or agreed to be made; and when such apportionment shall so be made it shall be binding on all under-lessees and other persons and corporations whatsoever, whether parties to the said agreement or not.

Liabilities of tenants, and remedies of landlords, as to the lands not conveyed.

2. And be it enacted, that in case of any such apportionment as aforesaid, and after the lands so conveyed or agreed to be conveyed as aforesaid shall have been conveyed, the lessee, and all parties entitled under him to the lands comprised in the lease not included in such conveyance, shall, as to all future accruing rent, and of all future fines certain or fixed sums of money, to be paid upon renewals, be liable only to so much of the rent and of such fines or sums of money as shall be apportioned in respect of such last-mentioned lands; and the party entitled to the rent reserved by the lease shall have all the same rights and remedies for the recovery of such portion of the rent as last aforesaid as previously to such apportionment he had for the recovery of the whole rent reserved by such lease; and all the covenants, conditions, and agreements of such lease, except as to the amount of rent to be paid, and of fines or sums of money to be paid upon renewals, in case of any apportionment of the same respectively, shall remain in force with regard to that part of the land comprised in the lease which shall not be so conveyed as aforesaid, in the same manner as they would have done in case such part only of the land had been included in the lease.

The same person may grant several sites for schools in the same parish if the whole extent do not exceed certain limits. 4 & 5 Vict. c. 38, s. 9.

3. And whereas by the said first-recited Act power is given to any person or corporation to grant any number of sites for distinct and separate schools; but after providing that the site of each school and residence do not exceed one acre, it is also provided that not more than one such site shall be in the same parish; and doubts have been entertained as to the meaning of this last-recited proviso: be it therefore declared and enacted, that nothing in the said Act contained shall prevent any person or corporation from granting any number of sites for separate and distinct schools in the same parish, provided the aggregate quantity of land granted by such person in the same parish shall not exceed the extent of one acre.

4. And whereas it would be expedient that the absolute owners of land and tenants in tail in possession should have the power of granting land to a limited extent for the purpose of erecting sites for schools to be applied and used in and for the education and instruction of persons intended to be masters or mistresses of elementary schools for poor persons, without any risk of such grant being defeated by the death of the grantor: Be it therefore enacted, that it shall be lawful for all persons, being such absolute owners or tenants in tail in possession as aforesaid, to grant, convey, or enfranchise, by way of gift, sale, or exchange, any quantity of land, not exceeding in the whole five acres, to any corporation sole or aggregate, or to several corporations sole, or to any trustees whatsoever, to be held, applied, and used by such corporation or corporations or trustees in and for the erection of school buildings and premises thereon for the purpose of educating and instructing, and of boarding during the time of such education and instruction, persons intended to be masters or mistresses of elementary schools for poor persons, and for the residence of the principal or master or mistress and other officers of such institution; and such gift, sale, or exchange shall be and continue valid, if otherwise lawful, although the donor or grantor shall die within twelve calendar months from the execution thereof: Provided always, that it shall be lawful for the trustees of such school buildings and premises to allow the same to be applied and used, concurrently with the education and instruction of such masters or mistresses, for the purpose of boarding other persons, and of educating and instructing the said persons in religious and useful knowledge.

Grants of land for sites of schools by owners or tenants in tail to be valid, although grantor die within twelve months.

5 And whereas the absolute owners of land may grant, subject to the regulations and provisions prescribed by the statutes in such behalf, any quantity of such land to trustees, to be held upon charitable purposes; and it would be beneficial that they should be authorized to exercise such power in respect of lands granted for the sites or for the endowment of the last-mentioned schools, or of schools for poor persons, by vesting the same so as to secure it permanently for the purpose of the trust, without the necessity of subsequent renewals of the deeds of trust: Be it therefore enacted, that where any such person shall be lawfully entitled to convey an estate in land

The owners of land empowered to vest any quantity of land for purposes of these Acts in corporations.

to trustees, to hold the same upon any charitable use, and shall be desirous of conveying the same for the purposes of the Acts hereinbefore referred to, or this Act, or for the endowment of such schools, such person may grant and convey the same to any corporation or corporations as aforesaid, to be held in trust for such purposes, whatever may be the quantity of land or extent of the estate so to be granted and conveyed.

Mode of conveying the lord's interest and that of the copyholder in copyhold land.

6. And be it enacted, that where land of copyhold or customary tenure shall have been or shall be granted for the purposes of the said Acts, the conveyance of the same by any deed wherein the copyholder shall grant and convey his interest, and the lord shall also grant his interest, shall be deemed to be valid and sufficient to vest the freehold interest in the grantee or grantees thereof without any surrender or admittance or enrolment in the Lord's Court.

Interpretation clause.

7. And be it enacted, that, except in cases where there shall be something in the subject or context repugnant to such construction, words occurring in this Act and the above-recited Acts importing the singular number shall include the plural number, and words importing the plural number shall include the singular number; and words importing the masculine gender only shall include females; and the word "land" shall include messuages, houses, lands, tenements, hereditaments, and heritages of every tenure; and the word "lease" shall include an under-lease, agreement for a lease, and missive of lease; and the word "owner" shall include any person or corporation enabled under the provisions of the said firstly-hereinbefore-mentioned Act to convey lands for the pur-es thereof.

Act may be amended, &c.

8. And be it enacted, that this Act may be amended or repealed by any Act to be passed in this present session of parliament.

14 & 15 VICT. CAP. 24.

An Act to amend the Acts for the granting of Sites for Schools.

[24th July, 1851.]

WHEREAS by the statute fourth and fifth Victoria, chapter thirty-eight, power is given to divers persons therein mentioned to grant, convey, and enfranchise a certain portion of land for the purpose of a site for a school for the education of poor persons, or for the residence of a schoolmaster or schoolmistress, or otherwise for the education of poor persons in religious and useful knowledge, and provisions are contained therein for facilitating the conveyance of such sites and perpetuating the trusts of the deeds: And whereas the persons therein mentioned having been authorized to grant any number of sites for distinct and separate schools, and residences for the master or mistress thereof, it is provided that the site of each school and residence should not exceed the extent of one acre, and it is also provided that not more than one such site should be in the same parish: And whereas by the twelfth and thirteenth Victoria, chapter forty-nine, it is declared and enacted, that nothing in the last-recited Act contained should prevent any person or corporation from granting any number of sites for separate and distinct schools in the same parish, provided the aggregate quantity of land granted by such person in the same parish should not exceed the extent of one acre: And whereas by reason of the great extent of some parishes, wherein the population is very large, this limitation is found to be productive of inconvenience, and to prevent the extension of the education of the poor; and it is desirable to make further provision in this behalf: Be it therefore enacted by the Queen's most excellent Majesty, by and with the advice and consent of the Lords spiritual and temporal, and Commons, in this present parliament assembled, and by the authority of the same, as follows:

1. The word parish in the sections of the statutes herein referred to shall, in the case of any parish which The word parish in the 4 & 5 Vict.

c. 38, s. 9, and 12 & 13 Vict. c. 49, s. 3, to signify an ecclesiastical district in any divided parish.

has heretofore been or shall hereafter be divided by lawful authority into two or more ecclesiastical districts, whether confined to such parish, or comprising also any part of another parish, be construed with reference to such parish to signify each such ecclesiastical district.

Incorporation of this Act with recited Acts.

2. This Act shall be construed as and be deemed to be a part of the said recited Acts, except so far as it amends the same.

II.—Provisions of Charitable Trusts Acts, 1853 to 1869, which relate to the Sale, Leasing, and Exchange of Lands belonging to any Charity (*a*).

16 & 17 VICT. CAP. 137.

An Act for the better Administration of Charitable Trusts.

[20th August, 1853.]

* * * * *

Board may sanction building leases, working mines, doing repairs and improvements;

21. If in any case it appear to the trustees or persons for the time being acting in the administration or management of any charity, or the estates or property thereof, that any part of the charity lands or estates may be beneficially let on building, repairing, improving or other leases, or on leases for working any mine, or that the digging for or raising of stone, clay, gravel, or other minerals, or the cutting of timber, would be for the benefit of the charity, or that it would be for the benefit of such charity that any new road or street should be formed or laid out, or any drains or sewers made through any part of the charity estates, or that any new building should be erected, or that any existing building should be repaired, altered, rebuilt, or wholly removed, or that any other improvements or alterations in the state or condition of the lands or estates of such charity should be made, it shall be lawful for such trustees or persons to lay before the said board a statement and proposal in relation to any of the matters aforesaid: and it shall be lawful for the said board, if they think that the leases or acts to which the statement and proposal relate, (with or

---

(*a*) See section 20, *ante*, p. 20, and section 78, *ante*, p. 67.

without modifications or alterations) would be beneficial to the charity, to make such order under their seal for and in relation to the granting of such leases, or the doing of any other such acts as aforesaid, and any circumstances connected therewith, as they may think fit, although such leases or acts respectively shall not be authorized or permitted by the trust; and the said board, by any such order, may authorize the application of any monies or funds belonging to the charity for any of the purposes or acts aforesaid, and, if necessary, may authorize the trustees to raise any sum of money by mortgage of all or any part of the charity estates; *provided that compulsory provisions be reserved in every such mortgage for the payment of the principal money borrowed by annual instalments, and for the redemption and reconveyance of the mortgaged estates, within the period of not more than thirty years.*

and may authorize the application of the charity funds or the raising of money on mortgage for those purposes.

* * * * *

Board, under special circumstances, may authorize sale or exchange of charity lands.

24. Upon application to the said board by the trustees or persons acting in the administration of any charity, representing to the said board that, under the special circumstances of any land belonging to the charity, a sale or exchange of such land can be effected on such terms as to increase the income of the charity, or would otherwise be advantageous to the charity, such board may, if they think fit, inquire into such circumstances, and if after inquiry they are satisfied that the proposed sale or exchange will be advantageous to the charity may authorize the sale or exchange, and give such directions in relation thereto, and for securing the due investment of the money arising from any such sale, or by way of equality of exchange for the benefit of the charity, as they may think fit.

Board may authorize the redemption of rent-charges.

25. The said board shall have authority, upon such application as aforesaid, to authorize the sale to the owners of the land charged therewith of any rentcharge, annuity, or other periodical payment charged upon land, and payable to or for the benefit of any charity, or applicable to charitable purposes, upon such terms and conditions as they may deem beneficial to the charity, and to give such directions for securing the due investment of the money arising from such sale for the benefit of the charity, or for securing the due application thereof to

such charitable purposes as they may think fit; and in like manner the trustees of any charity, with the consent of the board, may purchase any rentcharge or other yearly payment to which the charity estate is or shall be liable.

Leases, sales, &c. authorized by the board to be valid.

26. The leases, sales, exchange, and other transactions authorized by such board under the powers of this Act shall have the like effect and validity as if they had been authorized or directed by the express terms of the trust affecting the charity.

Trustees of charities enabled to purchase sites for building from owners under disability, &c., according to the provisions of Lands Clauses Consolidation Act, 1845

27. Where any land shall be required for the erection or construction of any house or building, with or without garden, playground, or other appurtenances, for the purposes of any charity, *and the trustees of the charity shall be legally authorized to purchase and hold such land*, but by reason of the disability of any person having an estate or interest in such land, or of any defect in title thereto, a valid and perfect assurance of the same land cannot be made to the trustees of the charity in the ordinary manner, it shall be lawful for the trustees of the charity, with the sanction of the said board (such sanction to be certified under the hand of their secretary), to take and purchase such land according to the provisions of "The Lands Clauses Consolidation Act, 1845;" and for that purpose all the clauses and provisions of the last-mentioned Act with respect to the purchase of lands by agreement, and with respect to the purchase money or compensation coming to parties having limited interests, or prevented from treating, or not making a title, and also with respect to conveyances of lands, so far as the same clauses and provisions respectively are applicable to the cases contemplated by this provision, shall be incorporated in this Act; and in all cases cases contemplated by this provision the expression "the Special Act," used in the said clauses and provisions of the said "Lands Clauses Consolidation Act," shall be construed to mean this Act; and the expression "the promoters of the undertaking," used in the same clauses and provisions, shall be construed to mean the trustees of the charity in question.

18 & 19 VICT. CAP. 124.

An Act to amend the Charitable Trusts Act, 1853.

[14th August, 1855.]

* * * * *

16. The acting trustees of every charity, or the majority of them, provided that such majority do not consist of less than three persons, shall have at law and in equity power to grant all such leases or tenancies of land belonging thereto, and vested in the official trustee of charity lands, as they would have power to grant in the due administration of the charity if the same land were legally vested in themselves; and all covenants, conditions, and remedies contained in or incident to any lease or tenancy so granted shall be enforceable by and against the trustees or persons acting in the administration of the charity for the time being, and their alienees or assigns, in like manner as if such lands had been legally vested in the trustees granting such lease or tenancy at the time of the execution thereof, and had legally remained in or had devolved to such trustees or administrators for the time being, their alienees or assigns, subject to the same lease or tenancy.

Power to acting trustees to grant leases.

* * * * *

29. It shall not be lawful for the trustees or persons acting in the administration of any charity to make or grant, otherwise than with the express authority of parliament, under any Act already passed or which may hereafter be passed, or of a court or judge of competent jurisdiction, or according to a scheme legally established, or with the approval of the board, any sale, mortgage, or charge of the charity estate, or any lease thereof in reversion after more than three years of any existing term, or for any term of life, or in consideration wholly or in part of any fine, or for any term of years exceeding twenty-one years.

Restrictions of charges and leases of charity estates.

* * * * *

32. The board may authorize the application of any

Board may authorize

payment for equality of exchange or partition.

funds belonging to any charity in payments for equality of exchange or partition, or in payment of any expenses incident thereto, or may authorize the trustees to raise any money for such purposes by mortgage of any land acquired on such exchange or partition, or belonging to the charity.

* * * * *

Expenses of exchanges and partitions, and determining application of charges.

34. The expenses incident to the application for and procuring of any such order of exchange or partition, or order determining the land charged with any rent, annuity, or periodical payment, shall be paid by the trustees or administrators of the charity, or by the other parties to such transactions, or by both, as the board may direct.

Incorporated charities and trustees for charities may re-invest in land.

35. Any incorporated charity, or the trustees of any charity, whether incorporated or not, may, with the consent of the board, invest money arising from any sale of land belonging to the charity, or received by way of equality of exchange or partition, in the purchase of land, and may hold such land, or any land acquired by way of exchange or partition, for the benefit of such charity, without any licence in mortmain.

Order of board for investments to be carried into effect, and cost to be raised.

36. All orders of the board for the investment of money coming to any charity, or the trustees thereof on any sale, exchange, or partition, shall be carried into effect by the trustees or persons administering the charity; and all monies which the board shall order to be provided out of any income or property of a charity for the payment of the costs of any such transaction shall be provided or raised by the trustees or administrators of the charity, and applied accordingly.

Board may direct official trustees to convey lands, &c.

37. It shall be lawful for the board to authorize or order and direct the official trustee of charity lands and the official trustees of charitable funds respectively to convey lands, and to assign, transfer, and pay over stocks, funds, monies, and securities, as the board shall think expedient.

Leases, &c. to be valid, notwith-

38. All leases, sales, exchanges, partitions, and transactions authorized by the board under the principal Act

or this Act shall be valid and effectual, notwithstanding the Act of the thirteenth year of the reign of Queen Elizabeth, chapter ten, the Acts of the fourteenth year of the same Queen, chapters eleven and fourteen, the Acts of the eighteenth year of the same Queen, chapters six and eleven, the Act of the thirty-ninth year of the same Queen, chapter five, and the Act of the twenty-first year of the reign of King James the First, chapter one, or any disabling Act applicable to the charity the estates whereof shall be the subject of any such transaction. standing disabling Acts.

39. It shall be lawful for the board to prepare, and under their seal to approve of, any scheme for the letting of the property or any part of the property of any charity; and all leases granted by any trustees or persons acting in the management of any charity, pursuant to or in conformity with such scheme, shall be valid. Board may approve schemes for letting charitable property.

* * * * *

41. Section twenty-seven of "The Charitable Trusts Act, 1853," shall be construed and operate as if the words "and the trustees of the charity shall be legally authorized to purchase and hold such land" had been omitted therefrom; and incorporated trustees of any charity shall be competent to purchase and hold lands for the purposes mentioned in the same section without licence in mortmain. Construction of sect. 27 of 16 & 17 Vict. c. 137.

---

23 & 24 VICT. CAP. 136.

An Act to amend the Law relating to the administration of endowed Charities.

[28th August, 1860.]

* * * * *

15. The power vested in the said board by the twenty-first section of "The Charitable Trusts Act, 1853," of authorizing the application of monies belonging to any charity, or to be raised on the security of the properties Sect. 21 of 16 & 17 Vict. c. 137 extended.

thereof, to the improvement of such properties, shall extend to authorize the application of any like monies to any other purpose or object which the board shall consider to be beneficial to the charity or the estate or objects thereof, and which shall not be inconsistent with the trusts or intentions of the foundation.

---

25 & 26 VICT. CAP. 112.

An Act for establishing the Jurisdiction of the Charity Commissioners in certain Cases.

[7th August, 1862.]

WHEREAS by the Acts relating to the charity commissioners for England and Wales authority has been given to the commissioners to make orders for various purposes in charity cases upon summary application, and particularly in relation to the appointment and removal of trustees, and the sale, exchange, leasing, and improvement of the property of charities: And whereas in various private Acts of Parliament and decrees and orders of the High Court of Chancery relating to charities such powers and authorities are often given or reserved, with directions that the same shall be exercised by the said court, or with its sanction or approbation, and doubts are entertained whether in such cases the authority given to the charity commissioners can be validly exercised: Be it therefore enacted and declared by the Queen's most excellent Majesty, by and with the advice and consent of the Lords spiritual and temporal, and Commons, in this present present Parliament assembled, and by the authority of the same, as follows:

No provision in any Act of parliament, or decree relating to any charity under any order of the Court of Chancery, to exclude any jurisdiction

1. No provision contained in any such Act of Parliament or decree or order as aforesaid for the appointment or removal of trustees of any charity, or for or relating to the sale, exchange, leasing, disposal, or improvement of any property, by or under the order or with the approval of the Court of Chancery, shall (in the absence of any express direction to the contrary, to be contained in any future Act of Parliament, order, or decree,) exclude or impair any jurisdiction or authority which might

otherwise be properly exercised for the like purposes by the charity commissioners for England and Wales.

which might otherwise be exercised by charity commissioners.

---

32 & 33 VICT. CAP. 110.

An Act for Amending the Charitable Trusts Acts.
[11th August, 1869.]

*   *   *   *   *

Legal power of majority of trustees to deal with charity estates.

12. Where the trustees or persons acting in the adminis tration of any charity have power to determine on any sale, exchange, partition, mortgage, lease, or other disposition of any property of the charity, a majority of those trustees or persons who are present at a meeting of their body duly constituted and vote on the question shall have and be deemed to have always had full power to execute and do all such assurances, acts, and things as may be requisite for carrying any such sale, exchange, partition, mortgage, lease, or disposition into effect, and all such assurances, acts, and things shall have the same effect as if they were respectively executed and done by all such trustees or persons for the time being and by the official trustee of charity lands.

III. Incorporated provisions of "The Metropolis Management Act, 1855," and "The Metropolis Management Amendment Act, 1862," (*a*)

18 & 19 VICT. CAP. 120.

An Act for the better Local Management of the Metropolis.
[14th August, 1855.]

*   *   *   *   *

Churchwardens to appoint persons

14. Where any parish is divided into wards, the churchwardens, three clear days at least before the day of election, shall appoint in writing under their hands a

---

(*a*) See section 37, subsection (6), *ante*, p. 34.

to preside at ward elections.

person to preside at such election as aforesaid in each of the said wards, except any ward in which one of the churchwardens shall preside, and notify such appointment to the vestry clerk of the parish.

Rate collectors to assist at the elections.

15. The rate collectors, or persons appointed by them, shall attend the churchwardens and persons presiding at elections under this Act, and inspectors of votes, to assist in ascertaining that the persons presenting themselves to vote are parishioners rated to the relief of the poor in the parish, or the respective wards thereof, and duly qualified to vote at the election.

Form of proceeding at elections.

16. On the day of election of vestrymen and auditors in any parish under this Act the parishioners then rated to the relief of the poor in the parish, or, where the parish is divided into wards under this Act, in the ward thereof for which the election is holden, and who are desirous of voting, shall meet at the place appointed for such election, and shall then and there nominate two ratepayers of the parish, or (if the parish be divided into wards) of the ward for which the election is holden, as fit and proper persons to be inspectors of votes; and the churchwardens, or, in the case of a ward election, such one of the churchwardens as is present thereat, or where one of the churchwardens is not present, the person appointed by them to preside thereat, shall, immediately after such nomination as aforesaid by the parishioners, nominate two other such ratepayers to be such inspectors; and after such nominations the said parishioners shall elect such persons duly qualified as may be there proposed for the offices of vestrymen and auditors or auditor; and the chairman at such meeting shall declare the names of the parishioners who have been elected by a majority of votes at such meeting: Provided nevertheless, that no person shall be entitled to join or vote in any such election for any parish, or any ward of any parish, or be deemed a ratepayer thereof, or be entitled to do any act as such under this Act, unless he have been rated in such parish to the relief of the poor for one year next before the election, and have paid all parochial rates, taxes and assessments due from him at the time of so voting or acting, except such as have been made or become due within six months immediately preceding such voting or acting.

17. Provided always, that any five ratepayers may then and there, in writing or otherwise, demand a poll, which shall be taken by ballot on the day next following; and shall commence at eight of the clock in the forenoon and close at such hour as hereinafter mentioned; that is to say, at six of the clock in the afternoon in the case of any election to be holden in November, 1855, and at eight of the clock in the afternoon in all other cases; each ratepayer depositing as hereinafter provided two folded papers, one of which papers shall contain the names of the persons for whom such parishioner may vote as fit and proper to be members of the vestry, and the other shall contain the names or name of the persons or person for whom such parishioner may vote as fit and proper to be auditors or auditor of accounts; and each ratepayer shall have one vote and no more for the members of the vestry, and one vote and no more for the auditors or auditor of accounts to be chosen in the said parish or ward. Power to demand a poll, which shall be taken by ballot.

18. The persons voting shall deposit such folded papers in two separate sets of balloting glasses or boxes, one set for voting papers for members of vestry, and another set for the voting papers for auditors or an auditor; and the said balloting glasses or boxes shall be closed at the time hereinbefore fixed for the closing of the poll; and the inspectors for the parish or ward (as the case may be) shall forthwith meet together, and proceed to examine the said votes, and if necessary shall continue the examination by adjournments from day to day, not exceeding two days (Sunday excepted), until they have decided upon the persons duly qualified according to the provisions of this Act who may have been chosen to fill the aforesaid offices. Duty of inspectors of votes.

19. In case an equality of votes appear to the aforesaid inspectors to be given for any two or more persons to fill either of the said offices, the inspectors shall decide by lot upon the person to be chosen. Provision for case of equality of votes.

* * * * *

21. If any person knowingly personate and falsely assume to vote in the name of any parishioner entitled to vote in any election under this Act, or forge or in any way Penalty for forging or falsifying any voting paper or

obstructing the election.

falsify any name or writing in any paper purporting to contain the vote or votes of any parishioner voting in any such election, or by any contrivance attempt to obstruct or prevent the purposes of any such election, the person so offending shall, upon conviction before any two or more justices of the peace having jurisdiction in the parish, be liable to a penalty of not less than 10*l.* and not more than 50*l.*, and in default of payment thereof shall be imprisoned for a term not exceeding six nor less than three months.

A list of persons elected vestrymen and auditors by parishioners to be published.

22. The inspectors shall, immediately after they have decided upon whom the aforesaid elections have fallen, deliver to the churchwardens, or to one of them, or other the person presiding at the election, a list of the persons chosen by the parishioners to act as vestrymen and auditors or an auditor of accounts; and the said list, or a copy thereof, shall be published in the parish as herein provided.

Penalty on inspector for making incorrect return.

23. If any inspector wilfully make or cause to be made an incorrect return of the said votes, every such offender shall, upon information laid by any person before two or more justices of the peace having jurisdiction in the parish, and upon conviction for such offence, be liable to a penalty of not less than 25*l.* and not exceeding 50*l.*

Vestries to provide places for holding elections, and pay expenses of taking poll, &c.

24. The vestry of every parish mentioned in either of the schedules (A.) and (B.) to this Act shall provide such places as may be requisite for holding elections of vestrymen and auditors under this Act, and taking the poll thereat; and the expenses of providing such places, of publishing notices, of taking the poll, and of making the return at elections of vestrymen and auditors, shall be paid out of the poor rates of the parish by order of the vestry: Provided always, that the places requiring to be provided for the first election under this Act of vestrymen and auditors in any parish shall be provided by the churchwardens, and the expenses of providing the same shall be paid out of the poor rates, upon their order.

As to parishes having

25. The provisions hereinbefore contained shall, so far as concerns any parish in either of the said schedules

(A.) and (B.) in which there are no churchwardens, be construed as referring to the overseers of the poor instead of the churchwardens.

no church-wardens.

How notices and lists to be published.

26 Every notice and list hereinbefore required to be published in any parish or ward of any parish shall be so published by being fixed in some public and conspicuous situation, on the outside of the outer door or outer wall near the door of every church and public chapel in such parish or ward, including places of public worship which do not belong to the Established Church, and if there be no such building as aforesaid, then in some public and conspicuous situation within such parish or ward.

Churchwardens, &c., not complying with Act guilty of misdemeanor.

27. If any churchwarden, overseer, rate collector, or other parish officer refuse or neglect to call any meeting, or give any notice, or do any other act required of him under the provisions of this Act, he shall be deemed guilty of a misdemeanor.

* * * * * *

Payment to be obtained from the city and from parishes by precepts to the chamberlain of the city and to vestries and district boards.

172. For obtaining payment of the sums so assessed upon the city of London and the parishes mentioned in schedules (A) and (B.) to this Act, the said board shall issue precepts under their seal, requiring payment thereof to their treasurer, or into any bank therein mentioned, within such time as may be therein limited, and every such precept for any sum assessed upon the city of London shall be directed to the chamberlain of the said city; and every such precept for any sum assessed upon any parish mentioned in schedule (A.) to this Act shall be directed to the vestry thereof; and every such precept for any sum assessed upon any district mentioned in schedule (B.) to this Act, or any parish comprised therein, shall be directed to the board of works for such district; and where any such sum is assessed upon any part of any parish or district, the said metropolitan board shall specify in their precept the part of such parish or district upon which such sum is assessed.

Payment of sums assessed

173. The chamberlain of the city of London shall, out of any monies in the chamber of the said city pay

upon the city.

to the treasurer of the metropolitan board of works, or otherwise as they may direct, the sums required by their precepts, within such time as may be therein mentioned; and all payments so made by the said chamberlain shall be charged by him against and reimbursed to him out of any rates which the commissioners of sewers of the city of London are authorized to direct to be made under any Act relating to the sewerage of the said city; and such commissioners shall have full power to raise every such sum by any such rate which they may be authorized to direct to be made as aforesaid, or by any addition thereto.

Payment by vestries and district boards of sums assessed by metropolitan board.

174. All sums which any vestry or district board may be required to pay by such precepts as aforesaid shall be paid by such vestry and board respectively within such time as may be therein mentioned, and shall be raised in like manner as if the same were required by the said vestry or board for defraying the expenses of such vestry or board in the execution of their powers and duties under this Act in relation to the sewerage of their parish or district.

---

25 & 26 VICT. CAP. 102.

An Act to amend the Metropolis Local Management Acts.

[7th August, 1862.]

* * * * *

Payment of sums assessed upon places in said schedule (C.)

12. For obtaining payment of the sum assessed upon any place mentioned in schedule (C.) to the firstly recited Act for the metropolis main drainage rate, the said board shall issue a precept under their seal requiring payment of the amount mentioned in such precept to their treasurer, or into any bank therein mentioned, within such time or times as may be therein limited, and every such precept shall be directed to the masters of the bench, treasurer, governors, or other body or persons having the chief control or authority in any such place; and the

body or persons to whom any such precept shall be directed shall raise and levy the money required by the same by means of a separate rate, in like manner and subject to the like provisions as the sewers rate to be made under the provisions of the firstly recited Act and this Act; and the said body or persons may appoint one or more persons to collect any such rate, and may pay him or them such salary, poundage, or allowance as they may deem just and reasonable, and may take such security from every such collector for the due execution of his duty as they shall think reasonable and proper; and the several provisions hereinafter contained with respect to the levying, paying over, and accounting for monies levied by collectors by direction of any vestry shall be applicable to every such collector; and the several enactments with respect to the levying of monies by the said metropolitan board on the default of vestries and district boards shall apply in case of a default by the body or persons to whom any such precept may be directed by the said board to levy and pay over the money therein named according to the exigency thereof.

Metropolitan board may amend assessments and precepts where necessary.

13. It shall be lawful for the metropolitan board of works, in case of any omission or other inaccuracy in any assessment or precept which they have made or issued, to make such amendments or alterations therein as may render the same conformable to the provisions of the recited Acts and this Act; and it shall be lawful for the said board, should they deem it requisite and proper to revoke any precept which they may have issued, and to issue another precept in lieu thereof.

* * * * *

Inspectors of votes to appoint umpire.

36. The inspectors of votes directed to be appointed under the firstly-recited Act for any parish, or, where any parish is divided into wards, for any ward of a parish, may, before commencing the duties of their office under the said Act, appoint by writing under their hands an umpire; and in case the said inspectors shall be unable to agree upon or determine by a majority any matter which they are by the said Act required to determine, such matter shall be decided by the said umpire, and his decision in relation thereto shall be final and conclusive.

The Commissioners Clauses Act, 1847 (*a*).

10 VICT. CAP. 16.

An Act for consolidating in one Act certain provisions usually contained in Acts with respect to the constitution and regulation of bodies of commissioners appointed for carrying on undertakings of a public nature. [23rd April, 1847.]

* * * * *

AND with respect to the mortgages to be executed by the commissioners, be it enacted as follows:

Forms of mortgage.

75. Every mortgage or assignation in security of rates or other property authorized to be made under the provisions of this or the special Act shall be by deed duly stamped, in which the consideration shall be truly stated; and every such deed shall be under the common seal of the commissioners if they be a body corporate, or if they be not a body corporate shall be executed by the commissioners, or any five of them, and may be according to the form in the schedule (B.) to this Act annexed, or to the like effect; and the respective mortgagees or assignees in security shall be entitled one with another to their respective proportions of the rates and assessments or other property comprised in such mortgages or assignations respectively, according to the respective sums in such mortgages or assignations mentioned to be advanced by such mortgagees or assignees respectively, and to be repaid the sums so advanced, with interest, without any preference one above another by reason of the priority of advancing such monies, or of the dates of any such mortgages or assignations respectively.

Register of mortgages to be kept, and to be open to inspection.

76. A register of mortgages or assignations in security shall be kept by the clerk to the commissioners, and where by the special Act the commissioners are authorized or required to raise separate sums on separate rates or other property, a separate register shall be kept for each class of mortgages or assignations in security, and within fourteen days after the date of any mortgage or assignation in security an entry or memorial of the number and date thereof, and of the names of the parties thereto, with their proper additions, shall be made in the proper register, and every such register may be perused at all

(*a*) See section 57, *ante*, p. 47.

reasonable times by any person interested in any such mortgage or assignation in security without fee or reward.

77. Any person entitled to any such mortgage or assignation may transfer his right and interest therein to any other person, and every such transfer shall be by deed duly stamped, wherein the consideration shall be truly stated; and every such transfer may be according to the form in the schedule (C.) to this Act annexed, or to the like effect.

Transfers of mortgages.

78. Within thirty days after the date of every such transfer, if executed within the United Kingdom, or otherwise within thirty days after the arrival thereof in the United Kingdom, it shall be produced to the clerk to the commissioners, and thereupon such clerk shall cause an entry or memorial thereof to be made, in the same manner as in the case of the original mortgage or assignation in security, and for such entry the clerk may demand a sum not exceeding five shillings; and after such entry every such transfer shall entitle the transferee, his executors, administrators, or assigns, to the full benefit of the original mortgage or assignation in security, and the principal and interest thereby secured, and such transferee may in like manner assign or transfer the same again *toties quoties*, and it shall not be in the power of any person, except the person to whom the same shall have been last transferred, his executors, administrators, or assigns, to make void, release, or discharge the mortgage or assignation so transferred, or any money thereby secured.

Register of transfers to be kept.

79. Unless otherwise provided by any mortgage or assignation in security, the interest of the money borrowed thereupon shall be paid half-yearly to the several parties entitled thereto.

Interest on mortgages to be paid half yearly.

80. If the commissioners can at any time borrow or take up any sum of money at a lower rate of interest than any securities given by them and then be in force shall bear, they may borrow such sum at such lower rate as aforesaid, in order to pay off and discharge the securities bearing such higher rate of interest, and may charge the rates and other property which they may be authorized to mortgage or assign in security under this or the special Act, or any part thereof, with payment of such sum and such lower rate of interest, in such manner

Power to borrow money at a lower rate of interest to pay off securities at a higher rate.

and subject to such regulations as are herein contained with respect to other monies borrowed on mortgage or assignation in security.

Repayment of money borrowed at a time and place agreed upon.

81. The commissioners may, if they think proper, fix a period for the repayment of all principal monies borrowed under the provisions of this or the special Act, with the interest thereof, and in such case the commissioners shall cause such period to be inserted in the mortgage deed or assignation in security; and upon the expiration of such period the principal sum, together with the arrears of interest thereon, shall, on demand, be paid to the party entitled to receive such principal money and interest, and if no other place of payment be inserted in such deed such principal and interest shall be payable at the office of the commissioners.

Repayment of money borrowed when no time or place has been agreed upon.

82. If no time be fixed in the mortgage deed or assignation in security for the repayment of the money so borrowed, the party entitled to receive such money may, at the expiration or at any time after the expiration of twelve months from the date of such deed, demand payment of the principal money thereby secured, with all arrears of interest, upon giving six months previous notice for that purpose, and in the like case the commissioners may at any time pay off the money borrowed, on giving the like notice; and every such notice shall be in writing or print, or both, and if given by a mortgagee or creditor shall be delivered to the clerk or left at the office of the commissioners, and if given by the commissioners shall be given either personally to such mortgagee or creditor, or left at his residence, or if such mortgagee or creditor be unknown to the commissioners, or cannot be found after diligent inquiry, such notice shall be given by advertisement in the London Gazette if the office of the commissioners is in England, the Edinburgh Gazette if it is in Scotland, or in the Dublin Gazette if it is in Ireland.

Interest to cease on expiration of notice to pay off a mortgage debt.

83. If the commissioners shall have given notice of their intention to pay off any such mortgage or assignation in security at a time when the same may lawfully be paid off by them, then at the expiration of such notice all further interest shall cease to be payable thereon, unless, on demand of payment made pursuant to such notice, or at any time thereafter, the commissioners fail

to pay the principal and interest due at the expiration of such notice on such mortgage or assignation in security.

84. In order to discharge the principal money borrowed as aforesaid on security of any of the rates the commissioners shall every year appropriate and set apart out of such rates respectively a sum equal to the prescribed part, and if no part be prescribed one twentieth part of the sums so borrowed respectively, as a sinking fund to be applied in paying off the respective principal monies so borrowed, and shall from time to time cause such sinking fund to be invested in the purchase of exchequer bills or other government securities, or in Scotland deposited in one of the banks there incorporated by Act of Parliament or Royal Charter, and to be increased by accumulation in the way of compound interest or otherwise, until the same respectively shall be of sufficient amount to pay off the principal debts respectively to which such sinking fund shall be applicable, or some part thereof which the commissioners shall think ought then to be paid off, at which time the same shall be so applied in paying off the same in manner hereinafter mentioned.

Monies borrowed on security of rates to be paid off in a limited period.

85. Whenever the commissioners shall be enabled to pay off one or more of the mortgages or assignations in security which shall be then payable, and shall not be able to pay off the whole of the same class, they shall decide the order in which they shall be paid off by lot among the class to which such one or more of the mortgages or assignations in security belong, and shall cause a notice, signed by their clerk, to be given to the persons entitled to the money to be paid off, pursuant to such lot, and such notice shall express the principal sum proposed to be paid off, and that the same will be paid, together with the interest due thereon, at a place to be specified, at the expiration of six months from the date of giving such notice.

Mode of paying off mortgages.

86. Where by the special Act the mortgagees or assignees in security of the commissioners are empowered to enforce the payment of the arrears of interest, or the arrears of principal and interest, due to them, by the appointment of a receiver, then, if within thirty days after the interest accruing upon any such mortgage or assignation in security has become payable, and, after

Arrears of interest, when to be enforced by appointment of a receiver.

demand thereof in writing, the same be not paid, the mortgagee or assignee in security may, without prejudice to his right to sue for the interest so in arrear in any of the superior courts, require the appointment of a receiver, by an application to be made as herein-after provided; and if within six months after the principal money owing upon any such mortgage or assignation in security has become payable, and after demand thereof in writing the same be not paid, together with all interest due in respect thereof, the mortgagee or assignee in security, without prejudice to his right to sue for such principal money, together with all arrears of interest, in any of the superior courts, may, if his debt amount to the prescribed sum, alone, or if his debt do not amount to the prescribed sum he may in conjunction with other mortgagees or assignees in security, whose debts being so in arrear, after demand as aforesaid, together with his amount to the prescribed sum, require the appointment of a receiver, by an application to be made as herein-after provided.

Arrears of principal and interest.

As to the appointment of receiver.

87. Every application for a receiver in the cases aforesaid shall in England or Ireland be made to two justices, and in Scotland to the sheriff, and on any such application such justices or sheriffs may, by order in writing, after hearing the parties, appoint some person to receive the whole or a competent part of the rates or sums liable to the payment of such interest, or such principal and interest, as the case may be, until such interest, or until such principal and interest, as the case may be, together with all costs, including the charges of receiving the rates or sums aforesaid, be fully paid; and upon such appointment being made all such rates and sums of money as aforesaid, or such part thereof as may be ordered by the said justices or sheriff, shall be paid to the person so to be appointed, and the money so paid shall be so much money received by or to the use of the party to whom such interest, or such principal and interest, as the case may be, shall be then due, and on whose behalf such receiver shall have been appointed, and after such interest and costs, or such principal, interest, and costs, have been so received, the power of such receiver shall cease.

Account books to be

88. The books of account of the commissioners shall be open at all seasonable times to the inspection of the re-

spective mortgagees or assignees in security of the commissioners, with liberty to take extracts therefrom without fee or reward. open to the inspection of mortgagees.

SCHEDULE (B.) Sect. 75.

Form of Mortgage.

By virtue of [*here name the special Act*], we [*here name the corporation, if the commissioners be incorporated, or if not incorporated, five of the commissioners*, appointed in pursuance of the said Act, in consideration of the sum of paid to the treasurer to the said commissioners by *A.B.* of for the purposes of the said Act, do grant and assign unto the said *A.B.*, his executors, administrators, and assigns, such proportion of the rates, rents, profits, and other monies arising or accruing by virtue of the said Act from [*here describe the rates or other property proposed to be mortgaged*] as the said sum of doth or shall bear to the whole sum which is or shall be borrowed upon the credit of the said rates, rents, profits, or monies, to hold to the said *A.B.*, his executors, administrators, and assigns, from this day until the said sum of with interest at per centum per annum for the same, shall be fully paid and satisfied (the principal sum to be repaid at the end of years from the date hereof [*in case any period be agreed upon for that purpose*]). Given under our corporate seal [*or*, in witness whereof we have hereunto set our hands and seals, *or, if the deed be granted in Scotland, insert the testing clause required by the law of Scotland, as the case may be*], this day of one thousand eight hundred and

SCHEDULE (C.) Sect. 77.

Form of Transfer of Mortgage.

I *A. B.* of in consideration of the sum of paid to me by *C. D.* of do hereby transfer to the said *C. D.*, his executors, administrators, and assigns, a certain mortgage, [*or, if the deed be granted in Scotland*, a certain assignation in security,] number made by "The commissioners for executing the [*here name the special Act*] to bearing date the day of for securing the sum of and interest [*or, if such transfer be by endorsement*, the within security], and all my right, estate, and interest in and to the money thereby secured, and in and to the rates, rents, profits, or other monies thereby assigned. In witness whereof I have hereunto set my hand and seal [*or, if the deed be granted in Scotland, insert the testing clause required by the law of Scotland,*] this day of one thousand eight hundred and

---

V. Documentary Evidence (*a*).

31 & 32 VICT. CAP. 37.

An Act to Amend the Law relating to Documentary Evidence in Certain Cases.

[25th June, 1868.]

WHEREAS it is expedient to amend the law relating to evidence: Be it enacted by the Queen's most excellent Majesty, by and with the advice and consent of the Lords spiritual and temporal, and Commons, in this present parliament assembled, and by the authority of the same, as follows:

Short Title. 1. This Act may be cited for all purposes as "The Documentary Evidence Act, 1868."

Mode of proving certain documents. 2. *Primâ facie* evidence of any proclamation, order, or regulation issued before or after the passing of this Act by Her Majesty or by the privy council, also of any proclamation, order, or regulation issued before or after the passing of this Act by or under the authority of any such department of the government or officer as is mentioned in the first column of the schedule hereto, may be given in all courts of justice, and in all legal proceedings whatsoever, in all or any of the modes hereinafter mentioned; that is to say,

(1.) By the production of a copy of the Gazette purporting to contain such proclamation, order, or regulation:

(2.) By the production of a copy of such proclamation, order, or regulation purporting to be printed by the government printer. * * *

(3.) By the production, in the case of any proclamation, order, or regulation issued by Her Majesty or by the privy council, of a copy or extract purporting to be certified to be true by the clerk of the privy council or by any one of the lords or others of the privy council, and, in

(*a*) See section 83, *ante*, p. 70.

the case of any proclamation, order, or regulation issued by or under the authority of any of the said departments or officers, by the production of a copy or extract purporting to be certified to be true by the person or persons specified in the second column of the said schedule in connexion with such department or officer.

Any copy or extract made in pursuance of this Act may be in print or in writing, or partly in print and partly in writing.

No proof shall be required of the handwriting or official position of any person certifying, in pursuance of this Act, to the truth of any copy of or extract from any proclamation, order, or regulation.

* * * * *

4. If any person commits any of the offences following, that is to say, **Punishment of Forgery.**

(1.) Prints any copy of any proclamation, order, or regulation which falsely purports to have been printed by the government printer, * * * or tenders in evidence any copy of any proclamation, order, or regulation, which falsely purports to have been printed as aforesaid, knowing that the same was not so printed; or,

(2.) Forges or tenders in evidence, knowing the same to have been forged, any certificate by this Act authorized to be annexed to a copy of or extract from any proclamation, order, or regulation;

he shall be guilty of felony, and shall on conviction be liable to be sentenced to penal servitude for such term as is prescribed by the Penal Servitude Act, 1864, as the least term to which an offender can be sentenced to penal servitude, or to be imprisoned for any term not exceeding two years, with or without hard labour.

5. The following words shall in this Act have the meaning hereinafter assigned to them, unless there is something in the context repugnant to such construction; (that is to say,) **Definition of Terms.**

* * * * *

"Privy Council" shall include Her Majesty in council and the lords and others of Her Majesty's privy council, or any of them, and any com- **"Privy Council:"**

mittee of the privy council that is not specially named in the schedule hereto:

"Government Printer:" "Government Printer" shall mean and include the printer to Her Majesty: * * *

"Gazette." "Gazette" shall include the London Gazette, the Edinburgh Gazette, and the Dublin Gazette, or any of such Gazettes.

Act to be cumulative. 6. The provisions of this Act shall be deemed to be in addition to, and not in derogation of any powers of proving documents given by any existing statute or existing at common law.

SCHEDULE.

Column 1. Name of Department or Officer.	Column 2. Names of Certifying Officers.
The Commissioners of the Treasury.	Any Commissioner, Secretary, or Assistant Secretary of the Treasury.
The Commissioners for executing the Office of Lord High Admiral.	Any of the Commissioners for executing the Office of Lord High Admiral or either of the Secretaries to the said Commissioners.
Secretaries of State.	Any Secretary or Under-Secretary of State.
Committee of Privy Council for Trade.	Any member of the Committee of Privy Council for Trade or any Secretary or Assistant Secretary of the said Committee.
The Poor Law Board.	Any Commissioner of the Poor Law Board or any Secretary or Assistant Secretary of the said Board.
The Education Department. See 33 & 34 Vict. c. 75, sec. 83, *ante*, p. 69.	Any Member of the Education Department or any Secretary or Assistant Secretary of the Education Department. See 33 & 34 Vict. c. 75, sec. 83, *ante*, p. 69.

VI. Statutes relating to the Audit of Accounts (*a*).

Auditors' Powers and Duties.

7 & 8 Vict. c. 101, s. 32. Every auditor . . . . shall have full powers to examine, audit, allow, or disallow of accounts, and of items therein, relating to moneys assessed for and applicable to the relief of the poor of all parishes and unions within his district, and to all other money applicable to such relief; and such auditor shall charge in every account audited by him the amount of any deficiency or loss incurred by the neligence or misconduct of any person accounting, or of any sum for which any such person is accountable, but not brought by him into account against such person, and shall certify on the face of every account audited by him any money, books, deeds, papers, goods, or chattels, found by him to be due from any person; and when any such auditor has so certified any money, books, deeds, papers, goods, or chattels to be due from any person, he shall forthwith report the same to the said commissioners .

Books and Certified Balance.

Ib. And the person from whom any money is so certified to be due shall within seven days pay, or cause to be paid, such money to the treasurer of the guardians of the union or parish, if there be any such treasurer .

How to be applied.

All books, deeds, papers, goods, and chattels, and in the case where there is no treasurer as aforesaid, all moneys so certified to be due shall be delivered over or paid, within seven days of the same being certified, to the person or persons authorized to receive the same.

Recovery of Certified Balances, Books, &c.

Ib. And if any such money, books, deeds, papers, goods, or chattels, be not duly paid or delivered over as

(*a*) See section 60, subsection 6, *ante*, p. 52.

hereinbefore directed, the said auditor, or any auditor subsequently appointed, shall proceed, as soon as may be, to enforce the payment or delivering over the same; and all moneys so certified to be due by such auditor shall be recoverable as so certified from all or any of the persons making or authorizing the illegal payment, or otherwise answerable for such moneys, and shall be recovered on the application of such auditor, or of any such auditor subsequently appointed, or by any person for the time being entitled or authorized to receive the same, in the same manner as penalties and forfeitures may be recovered under the provisions of the said first-recited Act.

Penalty for refusing to deliver up Books, &c.

Ib. And if any person from whom any such books, deeds, papers, goods, or chattels may be due, neglect or refuse to deliver over the same to the person for the time being entitled or authorized to receive the same, the person so neglecting or refusing shall be liable, on the complaint of any such auditor for the time being, or of the person entitled or authorized to receive the same, to the penalties and proceedings provided in the case of overseers refusing or neglecting to pay and deliver over to their successors any sum or sums of money, goods, chattels, and other things in their hands.

Power of Auditor to require Declaration as to Accounts.

7 & 8 Vict. c. 101, s. 33. And it shall be lawful for any such auditor to require any person holden or accountable for any money, books, deeds, papers, goods, or chattels relating to the poor rate or the relief of the poor, to produce to such auditor his accounts and vouchers, and to make or sign a declaration with respect to such accounts.

Penalty for neglect to attend Audit.

Ib. And so often as such person neglects or refuses to attend, either at the audit or any adjournment thereof, when so required by such auditor, or to produce to him such accounts or vouchers, or any of them, or to make or sign a declaration with respect to his accounts, if thereunto required by such auditor, he shall be liable for every such refusal or neglect to forfeit forty shillings to be recovered as penalties and forfeitures under the said first-recited Act, or if he wilfully make or sign a false declaration in respect of such accounts, he shall be liable to the penalties of perjury.

Costs of Proceedings to enforce due Attendance at the Audit.

12 & 13 Vict. c. 103, s. 11. Where any auditor shall lay any information for a penalty in consequence of the default of any officer or other person to attend the audit, or the adjournment thereof, or to produce the proper account or vouchers, or to make or sign the proper declaration before him, the costs incurred by such auditor, when not recovered from the defendant in such information, shall, if the Poor Law Board consent thereto, be payable to such auditor, and be chargeable in like manner as the costs incurred by an auditor in enforcing the payment of sums certified by him to be due.

In what cases Notice of intended surcharge is to be given by Auditor.

11 & 12 Vict. c. 91, s. 8. If an auditor shall see cause to surcharge any person not liable by law to be surcharged by him, and to whom no notice is now required by law to be given, with any sum of money in reference to any payment considered by him to have been illegally or improperly made, he shall, if the person be not present at such audit, cause notice in writing of his intention to make such surcharge to be given, by post or otherwise, to the person against whom he shall purpose to make this surcharge, addressed to him at his last known place of abode, and shall adjourn the audit, so far as it shall relate to such particular matter, for a sufficient time to allow of such person appearing before him, and showing cause against such surcharge; and at such time the said auditor shall hear the party, if present, and determine according to the law and justice of the case.

Evidence in Proceedings by Auditors to recover Sums certified by them to be Due.

Ib. s. 9. In any proceedings to be taken by an auditor, or by his attorney, before justices, to recover sums certified by him to be due, it shall be sufficient for him —to produce a certificate of his appointment under the seal of the Poor Law Commissioners, or of the commissioners aforesaid—and to state and prove that the audit was held—that the certificate was made in the book of account of the union or parish to which the same relates —and that the sum certified to be due had not been paid to the treasurer of the guardians of the union or of the parish, as the case may require, within seven days after the same had been so certified, nor within three clear days before the laying of the information, of which nonpayment a certificate in writing, purporting to be signed by the treasurer, shall be sufficient proof on the part of the auditor;—and if at the hearing of such information it shall be proved that the said sum had been paid to the treasurer subsequently to the date of such last-mentioned certificate, the costs incurred by such auditor shall be paid by the party against whom the information shall be laid, unless he prove that notice of such payment had been given to the auditor twenty-four hours at least prior to the laying of the information.

Mode of certifying Balances by Auditors when the Officer continues in Office.

11 & 12 Vict. c. 91, s. 5. Where any overseer or officer shall be continuing in office at the time when the accounts are audited, the auditor shall certify as due such sums of money only as shall be disallowed or surcharged by him in the accounts so audited.

How when the Term of Office shall have expired.

Ib. But where the term of office of such overseer or officer shall have expired at the time when the accounts are audited, he shall ascertain the balance which he shall find to be then due on the accounts so audited, together with the sum (if any) which he shall have disallowed or surcharged, and shall give credit for all sums which shall be proved before him to have been paid in respect of such balance to the succeeding overseers or officers, or otherwise lawfully applied on behalf of the parish or union interested therein, before the date of his audit, and he shall certify, report, and recover, in the manner provided by law, the balance remaining due after such credit shall have been given.

Form of Certificate of Auditor.

Ib. And every certificate made by any auditor, if made according to the form set forth in the schedule hereunto annexed, or to the like effect, shall be deemed to be sufficient.

How when the sum disallowed does not amount to Forty Shillings.

Ib. Provided always, that where the sum or the aggregate of the sums disallowed by the auditor, in the account of any officer, shall not amount to forty shillings, the same may be paid over with the balance due from such officer, instead of being paid to the treasurer.

The following are the forms of certificates given in the schedule to the Act above referred to :—

1. *Against an accounting Officer.*

I do hereby certify, that in the account of *A. B.* the [*set out the name of the office*] of the parish of [*or* of the union], I have disallowed [*or* surcharged] the sum of .

As witness my hand, this day of , 18 .

M. N., auditor of the district, which comprises the above-named parish *or* union.

2. *Against a Person not an Accounting Officer.*

I do hereby certify, that in the accounts of the union [*or* of the parish of], I have disallowed the sum of £ . , as a payment illegally made out of the funds of such union [*or* parish], and I find that *C. D.* of , authorized the making of such illegal payment, and I do hereby surcharge the said *C. D.* with the same.

As witness my hand, this day of 18 .

M. N., auditor of the district, which comprises the above-named union *or* parish.

Limitation of Time upon Proceedings of Auditors for recovery of Money certified to be Due.

12 & 13 Vict. c. 103, s. 9. Whereas in the Act of the last session of parliament, intituled, "An Act to facilitate the performance of the duties of Justices of the Peace out of Sessions within England and Wales with respect to summary convictions and orders" (11 & 12 Vict. c. 43, s. 11), it is enacted, that in all cases where no time had then been or should thereafter be specially limited for making the complaints, or laying the informations therein referred to, every such complaint should be made and every such information laid within six calendar months from the time when the matter of such complaint or information respectively arose; and doubts have been entertained whether the provision aforesaid applies to proceedings by auditors to recover sums certified by them to be due in the accounts of officers or other persons, and it is desirable to remove such doubts: Be it therefore declared and enacted, that nothing in the provisions of the said Act herein recited shall be deemed to apply to any such proceeding by any auditor, but that no auditor shall commence any such proceeding after the lapse of nine calendar months from the disallowance or surcharge by such auditor, or, in the event of an application by way of appeal against the same to the Court of Queen's Bench or to the Poor Law Board, after the lapse of nine calendar months from the determination thereupon.

VII. Statutes relating to Appeals against Allowances, Disallowances, and Surcharges by Auditors (*a*).

Auditor on demand to state Reasons.

7 & 8 Vict. c. 101, s. 35. If any person aggrieved by any allowance, disallowance, or surcharge by any such auditor, require such auditor to state the reasons for the said allowance, disallowance, or surcharge, the auditor shall state such reasons in writing in the book of account in which the allowance, disallowance, or surcharge may be made.

Certiorari to remove Allowances or Disallowances into Court of Queen's Bench.

Ib. And it shall be lawful for every person aggrieved by such allowance, and for every person aggrieved by such disallowance or surcharge, if such last-mentioned person have first paid or delivered over to any person authorized to receive the same, all such money, goods, and chattels as are admitted by his account to be due from him or remaining in his hands, to apply to the Court of Queen's Bench for a writ of *certiorari* to remove into the said court the said allowance, disallowance, or surcharge, in the like manner and subject to the like conditions as are provided in respect of persons suing forth writs of *certiorari* for the removal of orders of the justices of the peace, except that the condition of such recognizance shall be, to prosecute such *certiorari* at the costs and charges of such person, without any wilful or affected delay; and if such allowance, disallowance, or surcharge, be confirmed, to pay to such auditor or his successor, within one month after the same may be confirmed, his full costs and charges, to be taxed according to the course of the said court; and except that the notice of the intended application, which shall contain a statement of the matter complained of, shall be given to such auditor or his successor, who shall in return to such writ return a copy under his hand of

(*a*) See section 60, subsection 6, *ante*, p. 52.

the entry or entries in such book of account to which such notice shall refer, and shall appear before the said court, and defend the allowance, disallowance, or surcharge, so impeached in the said court, and shall be reimbursed all such costs and charges as he may incur in such defence out of the poor rates of the union or parish respectively interested in the decision of the question, unless the said court make any order to the contrary.

Proceedings of the Court.

Ib. And on the removal of such allowance, disallowance, or surcharge, the said court shall decide the particular matter of complaint set forth in such statement, and no other; and if it appear to such court that the decision of the said auditor was erroneous, they shall, by rule of the court, order such sum of money as may have been improperly allowed, disallowed, or surcharged, to be paid to the party entitled thereto by the party who ought to repay or discharge the same.

Costs.

Ib. And they may also, if they see fit, by rule of the court, order the costs of the person prosecuting such *certiorari* to be paid by the parish or union to which such accounts relate, as to such court may seem fit; which rules of court respectively shall be enforced in like manner as other rules of the said court are enforceable.

Appeal to Poor Law Board.

Ib. s. 36. Provided always, that it shall be lawful for any person aggrieved as aforesaid by any allowance, or disallowance, or surcharge, in lieu of making application to the court of Queen's Bench for a writ of *certiorari*, to apply to the said commissioners to inquire into and decide upon the lawfulness of the reasons stated by the auditor for such allowance, disallowance, or surcharge, and it shall thereupon be lawful for the said commissioners to issue such order therein, under their hands and seal, as they may deem requisite for determining the question.

Appeal to the Equitable Jurisdiction of the Poor Law Board.

11 & 12 Vict. c. 91, s. 4. Where any appeal shall be made to the said commissioners against any allowance, disallowance, or surcharge, made by any auditor in the accounts of any guardians, overseers, or their officers, it shall be lawful for the said commissioners to decide the same according to the merits of the case; and if they shall find that any disallowance or surcharge shall have been or shall be lawfully made, but that the subject-matter thereof was incurred under such circumstances as make it fair and equitable that the disallowance or surcharge should be remitted, they may, by an order under their seal, direct that the same shall be remitted, upon payment of the costs, if any, which may have been incurred by the auditor or other competent authority in the enforcing of such disallowance or surcharge.

VIII. Table of Places within the Jurisdiction of the Metropolitan Board of Works under the Metropolis Local Management Act, 1855. See s. 3, *ante*, p. 1, and s. 39, *ante*, p. 37.

PARISHES, DISTRICTS, OR PARTS.	DIVISIONS, (See the 5th Schedule, *post.*)	Population Census, 1861.	Annual Rateable Value.	
			As per Poor Rate Basis, October, 1867.	As per County Rate Basis, or like Estimate, January, 1868.
Schedule (A.)			£	£
City of London	City	111,784	2,032,012	2,160,979
St. Marylebone	Marylebone	161,680	997,581	1,053,748
St. Pancras	Marylebone	198,788	1,024,927	925,872
St. Mary, Lambeth	Lambeth	162,044	698,444	770,000
St. George, Hanover Square	Westminster	87,711	882,724	1,076,272
St. Mary, Islington	Finsbury	155,341	808,543	777,632
St. Leonard, Shoreditch	Hackney	129,364	334,600	386,044
Paddington	Marylebone	75,784	691,306	758,344
St. Matthew, Bethnal Green	Hackney	105,101	224,778	192,116
St. Mary, Newington, Surrey	Lambeth	82,220	215,321	280,000
St. Giles, Camberwell	Lambeth	71,488	364,764	380,000
St. James, Westminster	Westminster	35,326	447,498	462,032
St. James and St. John, Clerkenwell	Finsbury	65,681	230,231	242,524
St. Luke's, Chelsea	Chelsea	63,439	263,462	299,868
St. Mary Abbott's, Kensingon	Chelsea	70,108	672,088	501,132
St. Luke, Middlesex	Finsbury	57,073	223,640	186,452
St. George-the-Martyr, Southwark	Southwark	55,510	151,372	175,000
St. Mary Magdalen Bermondsey	Southwark	58,355	216,868	234,000
St. George-in-the-East	Tower Hamlets	48,891	184,799	196,745
St. Martin-in-the-Fields	Westminster	22,689	284,655	265,336

	Hamlet of Mile End Old Town	Tower Hamlets	73,064	218,569	191,056
	Woolwich	Greenwich	41,695	87,816	96,000
	St. Mary, Rotherhithe	Southwark	24,502	110,594	126,000
	St. John, Hampstead		19,106	194,735	147,624
	Schedule (B.)				
Whitechapel District	St. Mary, Whitechapel	Tower Hamlets	37,454	131,378	127,426
	Christchurch, Spitalfields		20,593	55,852	47,636
	St. Botolph Without, Aldgate		4,000	41,370	44,865
	Holy Trinity, Minories		420	7,839	7,839
	Precinct of St. Katherine		208	17,000	17,272
	Hamlet of Mile End New Town		10,845	18,915	15,660
	Liberty of Norton Folgate		1,873	7,810	8,952
	Old Artillery Ground		2,168	5,469	4,675
	District of the Tower		1,409	4,055	3,423
Westminster District	St. Margaret	Westminster	67,890	461,932	339,660
	St. John-the-Evangelist				
Greenwich District	St. Paul, Deptford, including Hatcham	Greenwich	37,834	135,423	174,600
	St. Nicholas, Deptford		8,139	13,922	18,000
	Greenwich		40,002	146,160	148,220
Wandsworth District	Clapham		20,894	125,732	135,430
	Tooting Graveney		2,055	10,565	12,000
	Streatham		8,027	79,316	84,000
	St. Mary, Battersea, excluding Penge		19,600	172,308	190,420
	Wandsworth		13,346	96,299	97,870
	Putney, including Roehampton		6,481	55,347	64,500
Hackney District	Hackney	Hackney	76,687	440,875	323,192
	St. Mary, Stoke Newington	Finsbury	6,608	46,236	47,424

VIII. Table of Places within the Jurisdiction of the Metropolitan Board of Works under the Metropolis Local Management Act, 1855. See s. 3, *ante*, p. 1, and s. 39, *ante*, p. 37.

	PARISHES, DISTRICTS, OR PARTS.	DIVISIONS, (See the 5th Schedule, *post.*)	Population, Census, 1861.	Annual Rateable Value. As per Poor Rate Basis, October, 1867.	Annual Rateable Value. As per County Rate Basis, or like Estimate, January, 1868.
	Schedule (B.)—continued			£	£
St. Giles District	St. Giles-in-the-Fields .. .. .. St. George, Bloomsbury	Finsbury	540,76	252,219	277,412
Holborn District	St. Andrew, Holborn above Bars .. St. George the Martyr	Finsbury	32,251	132,460	141,280
	St. Sepulchre, Middlesex	..	4,609	19,716	17,488
	Liberty of Saffron Hill, &c...	..	7,148	27,072	31,697
	Liberty of Glasshouse Yard	..	1,455	4,235	4,154
Strand District	St. Anne, Soho	Westminster	17,426	83,357	96,236
	St. Paul, Covent Garden	.. ..	5,154	46,530	49,020
	Precinct of the Savoy	.. ..	380	8,142	9,112
	St. Mary-le Strand	.. ..	2,072	16,801	17,956
	St. Clement Danes	.. ..	15,592	85,078	95,676
	Liberty of the Rolls..	.. ..	2,274	19,107	18,808
Fulham District	St. Peter and St. Paul, Hammersmith ..	Chelsea ..	24,519	138,750	104,928
	Fulham	..	15,539	87,189	66,948
Limehouse District	St. Anne, Limehouse	Tower Hamlets ..	27,161	88,294	87,844
	St. John, Wapping	..	4,038	49,206	42,752
	St. Paul, Shadwell	..	8,499	41,095	42,648
	Hamlet of Ratcliff	..	16,874	51,024	61,560

District	Place	Borough			
Poplar District	All Saints, Poplar	Tower Hamlets	43,529	218,252	212,112
	St. Mary, Stratford-le-Bow		11,586	73,879	48,796
	St. Leonard, Bromley		24,081	97,828	83,412
St. Saviour's District	Christchurch	Southwark	17,069	61,388	67,000
	St. Saviour, including Liberty of The Clink		19,101	154,071	127,000
Plumstead District	Charlton next Woolwich	Greenwich	8,472	45,083	45,150
	Plumstead		24,502	57,346	57,350
	Eltham	.. ..	3,009	22,457	20,600
	Lee	.. ..	6,162	57,108	55,030
	Kidbrooke	.. ..	804	13,604	12,990
Lewisham District	Lewisham, including Sydenham Chapelry	.. ..	22,808	200,595	196,170
	Hamlet of Penge	.. ..	5,015	98,665	95,000
St. Olave's District	St. Olave	Southwark	6,197	76,874	71,000
	St. Thomas, Southwark		1,466	7,007	10,500
	St. John, Horselydown		11,393	50,326	59,500
	Schedule (C.)				
	EXTRA PAROCHIAL PLACES.				
Charterhouse		Finsbury	255	.. ..	1,948
Gray's Inn			308	.. ..	12,652
The Close of the Collegiate Church of St. Peter		Westminster	323	.. ..	1,456
Inner Temple		City	148	.. ..	19,866
Middle Temple			81	.. ..	13,000
Lincoln's Inn		Finsbury	47	.. ..	17,244
Staple Inn			42	.. ..	2,248
Furnival's Inn			202	.. ..	3,164
			28,808,944	16,019,895	16,196,547

IX. Circular of the Education Department on the Elementary Election Act, 1870.

FORM No. 70, August, 1870.

Education Department, 16th August, 1870.

Municipal borough of

SIR,—I am directed by the Lords of the Committee of Council on Education to request that you will take an early opportunity of calling the attention of the council of your borough to sections 67—72 of the "Elementary Education Act, 1870," and I am to beg that the requisite steps may be taken without delay for carrying out the provisions of these sections, with respect to the returns which the council (as the local authority of the district) are required to send to the education department, on or before the 1st day of January, 1871.

These returns will have to be made on two forms.

One of these, a general form, is intended to furnish certain information respecting the area contained within the municipal limits of the borough, which information the education department will have to take into consideration in deciding upon the school provision that will be required for the district. A copy of that form is enclosed.

The other, a special form, will have to be filled up by the managers or teacher of every school, whether public or private, within the same limits, which answers to the definition of an elementary school given in the third section of the Act. That section runs as follows:—

> "The term 'elementary school' means a school or department of a school at which elementary education is the principal part of the education there given, and does not include any school or department of a school at which the ordinary payments in respect of the instruction, from each scholar, exceed ninepence a week.

Some time will doubtless be occupied in obtaining all the information required for insertion in the general form. But with the view of having the special form filled up for each school, and returned to you in due time for the completion of the general form, it will be necessary to make immediate arrangements for ascertaining how many of these special forms you will require for elementary schools as above defined.

This is, therefore, the first point to be attended to; and my Lords earnestly beg that measures may be at once taken for ascertaining the number of elementary schools within the borough.

Your council will bear in mind that the education department, in determining the amount of public school accommodation for any district, are required to take into account not only schools in operation, but also those which, when completed, are likely to be efficient and suitable for the population. The promoters of those schools, therefore, which, though commenced, may not be finished on the day when the general return is sent in, will have to fill up, so far as circumstances permit, the same returns as will be made by the schools actually at work. Your preliminary enquiries must accordingly be extended to all the schools within the borough which at the date of your return are either—(1), in operation; or (2), in course of being supplied.

If you will fill up the enclosed schedule and return it to this department, as soon as you have ascertained the number of schools under these two heads, the requisite supply of forms will be sent to you.

I am, Sir,

Your obedient Servant,

F. R. Sandford,

Secretary.

To

The town clerk of the municipal borough of

Elementary Education Act, 1870.

FORM No. 72, August, 1870.

Municipal borough of

General return with respect to the population, rating, and school provision within the municipal limits of the borough.

N.B.—This return is to be strictly confined to the area within the municipal limits of the borough.

If any parish is divided by these limits, the part without the municipal area will be dealt with separately. This return is to include only the parts of such parishes *within that area.*

I. This borough, by the census of 1861, contained inhabitants.

II. It is estimated that the population now amounts to

III. The rateable value of the borough is
(i.) By the last valuation list dated £ *or,* if there is no such list,
(ii.) By the rate book now in force dated £

IV. The number of ratepayers, duly rated under the provisions of the Poor Rate Assessment and Collection Act, 1869, is

V. The number of elementary schools for which returns are herewith made to the education department is

(*a*) In operation

(*b*) In course of being supplied

N.B.—*It will be very convenient if you can forward with the return a map of the borough with the position of these schools marked upon it.*

VI. The number of the schools to which forms of return were delivered, but which have omitted, or refused, to fill them up is

A list of these schools is filed herewith.

I, the undersigned, town clerk of the borough of by the authority, and with the approval of the town council of the said borough, hereby certify to the completeness and accuracy of this general return.

Signed, this day of 1870.

____________________ Town Clerk.

____________________ (Address.)

INDEX.

www.ingramcontent.com/pod-product-compliance
Lightning Source LLC
Chambersburg PA
CBHW030835270326
41928CB00007B/1061

9783337218768